Scrapbooking

creating ★ scrapbooks, ★ albums, ★ journals,

and memory boxes

COUNTRY LIVING

Scrapbooking

creating scrapbooks, albums, journals, and memory boxes

★ text by Mary Caldwell

★ photography by Keith Scott Morton

★ styling by Amy Leonard

★ foreword by Nancy Mernit Soriano

Hearst Books

A Division of
Sterling Publishing Co., Inc.
New York

Produced by Smallwood & Stewart, Inc., New York City
Art Director: Debbie Sfetsios
Designer: Alexandra Maldonado
Editor: Carrie Chase
Crafts Editor: Deri Reed

Library of Congress Cataloging-in-Publication Data
Available upon request.

This book was previously published under the title
Country Living Handmade Scrapbooks.

10 9 8 7 6 5 4 3 2 1

Published by Hearst Books,
A Division of Sterling Publishing Co., Inc.
387 Park Avenue South, New York, N.Y. 10016

Country Living and Hearst Books are trademarks owned by
Hearst Magazines Property, Inc., in USA,
and Hearst Communications, Inc., in Canada.

Distributed in Canada by Sterling Publishing
C/o Canadian Manda Group, One Atlantic Avenue, Suite 105
Toronto, Ontario, Canada M6K 3E7
Distributed in Australia by Capricorn Link (Australia) Pty. Ltd.
P.O. Box 704, Windsor, NSW 2756 Australia

Manufactured in China

ISBN 1-58816-194-3

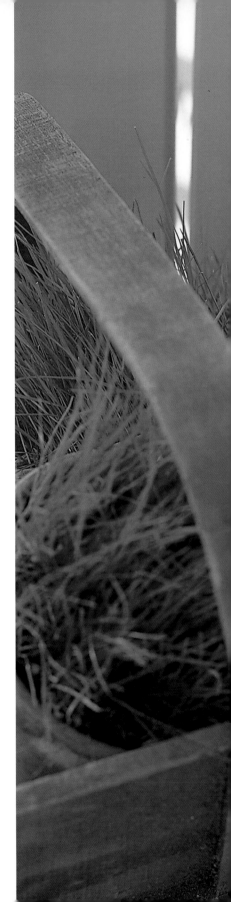

Our Wedding Day

Gifts from Nature

BOUQUET

BENEZRA AND PRINCE

Mead

HARMONY BOOKS

table of contents

foreword

We all want to hold on to important moments in our lives. A ticket stub from a favorite concert, photographs of a family reunion, a boarding pass from a trip abroad, a pressed flower from a special bouquet.

I have boxes at home filled with such treasures. Photos of my parents as children that have been passed down to me. Keepsakes from my own childhood that document the stages of my growing up. And now, a steady flow of new additions recording my son's development—his birth, first birthday, and first steps.

On the following pages, we offer a wealth of ideas and solutions on organizing, preserving, and displaying these special documents of our lives. We take a look at some very creative handmade scrapbooks, albums, journals, and keepsake boxes, and then give you advice on how to create your own personal remembrance. These projects have inspired me to look at my boxes and think about the most appropriate way to display and protect their contents. I'm sure these projects will have the same effect on you.

As we see our lives moving faster and faster, the need to document the special moments becomes even more important. It is a way for us to recall past experiences . . . to share them with family and friends . . . and perhaps pass them along to new generations.

— Nancy Mernit Soriano, Editor-in-Chief

chapter one

The favour of a reply is requested
before September 1, 1997

Ms. *Amy Brady*

allison

stuart

Table 14

materials and tools

Some time in the last several years, the word "scrapbook" underwent a dramatic grammatical conversion from noun to verb, as a whole new pastime emerged. In an age when we seem to be hurtling ever more rapidly into a technology-crammed future, people hungry for a link to the past and eager to create, with their own hands, a tangible memory bank of today have elevated "scrapbooking" to a unique art form. More than simply repositories of snapshots or newspaper clippings, today's scrapbooks combine the best, most intriguing elements of photo album, diary, and personal work of art.

Before you begin mulling over the projects in Chapter Two, take some time to acquaint yourself with the information on the following pages about typical materials, tools, and techniques used in scrapbooking. We cover choices in paper, albums, and related supplies, and also introduce some of the basics of mounting photos and embellishing pages, so that you can go on to use the projects as a point of departure for designing your own one-of-a-kind books.

CHOOSING A SCRAPBOOK

When you begin to scrapbook, one of the first decisions you'll have to make is selecting the right size and style of album or blank book. Take into account the materials you will be displaying, whether they are primarily flat or three-dimensional, photographs or mementos. Although the size, style, and shape of pages vary, most memory books and photo albums fit into a few basic categories:

◆ Ring-bound (loose-leaf) books—These range from standard school-issue three-ring binders to sophisticated leather-bound multi-ring arrangements. Ring-bound books lie flat

paper weights

Paper is rated by several things: Color, finish, and opacity are important. So is weight. The higher the pound rating, the heavier the paper. Some common weights are listed below:

Perforated computer paper: 15–18 lb.

Office-quality typing paper: 20 lb.

Good-quality stationery: 24 lb.

Brochure paper: 32 lb.

Medium cardstock: 67 lb.

Heavyweight cardstock: 110 lb.

for easy viewing and facilitate no-fuss rearranging of pages. In addition, if you plan to include memorabilia that's not flat, the rings will give the page some breathing room without stressing the binding. In use, pages mounted on O-shaped rings turn more easily than those in albums with D-shaped rings; in storage, D-shaped rings allow pages to line up squarely, putting less stress on them.

◆ Post-bound books—These are held together with small, hollow, two-part metal or plastic cylinders. One cylinder is inserted through the top of the punched pages, the other through the bottom; then the post is screwed together. Extension posts allow you to expand the number of pages in the book. Pages can be inserted or reordered, though not quite so conveniently as with ring binding.

◆ Spiral-bound books—Like their ring-bound counterparts, these lie open nicely, but the pages cannot be reordered. If you fill the first five pages of the album, only to discover another baby photo that should have gone earlier, you're out of luck unless you remove and repaste everything again.

◆ Sewn or perfect-bound blank books—Squared-off spines make these especially good journals or sketch books, but their tight bindings render them impractical for mounting more than a few items, or anything three-dimensional. Generally, sewn bindings are more durable than the glued bindings of a perfect-bound book.

Making Your Own Album

If you want to start from scratch, you can fashion covers from cardboard, bristol board, or mat board and cover them with paper, ribbon, or fabric. You can even go the bookbinding route and use bookbinding board and fabric to give your books a professional finish. Pages can be made of heavy cardstock, poster paper, heavy art paper, construction paper, or even corrugated cardboard. If you choose a lighter-weight paper, such as stationery or bond paper, you can reinforce and protect pages with sheet protectors, which are transparent sleeves that fit over the page. Make sure to purchase sheet protectors that are free of PVCs (polymers that can release gasses harmful to photographs).

PAPER POINTERS

The pages of your book are probably the second most important aspect of your project, after the binding style. And there is plenty of paper to choose from. If you can dream up a style of paper, chances are good that someone is already making it. Many craft, stationery, and photography supply stores carry an unbelievable array of albums and scrapbooks made from every conceivable kind of paper: You can

choose from pages that are smooth or textured, fancy-edged or plain, matte or glossy, solid or figured, blank or printed, or colored almost any hue of the rainbow. And if you are creating a book from scratch, the choices increase exponentially.

Nothing lasts forever, and paper degrades a lot faster than many other natural materials. Over time, chemical changes in the paper cause it to discolor, become brittle, and eventually crumble. Exposure to moisture, light, and temperature fluctuations as well as human handling contribute to decomposition, too, as can certain types of glue and tape. Paper that is acid-free and lignin-free may help improve the durability of your scrapbooking project, since it lacks the chief culprits in the demise of paper (lignin is a naturally occurring plant component that can contribute to paper's decomposition). Luckily, a lot of the available paper supplies, even those sold in nonprofessional stores, are acid-free.

To maximize the benefit of using acid-free paper, you must also use acid-free adhesive and decorations. And there is yet another consideration: Much of the memorabilia you choose to keep—such as newspaper clippings, greeting cards, or school papers—is likely to be acidic. Eventually, they too will yellow and become brittle. Over time, the acid can leech from the clipping into the paper on which it is mounted and compromise the integrity of the scrapbook. If you are most interested in enjoying the book in the here and now, don't let this dampen your fun; but there are a few common-sense steps that will help coax longevity from memorabilia, even if it falls far from being considered archival quality.

If the value—whether historic, sentimental, or monetary—of the items you are saving warrants it, you can choose one of several strategies to cope with acidic memorabilia:

◆ Use a deacidifying spray to treat the item before it is mounted. Read the product specifications carefully, and test it in an obscure spot; it won't work on everything.

acid test

If you're not sure whether your paper is acidic or not, you can test it with an inexpensive "pH tester" pen. It's like giving the item a litmus test. Draw a line with the pen in an inconspicuous spot on the paper. The color the line turns (this color varies depending on what brand pen you buy) will provide a rough idea of whether or not the the item is acidic. The pen works best on white (or off-white) paper; otherwise, the color may not be readily apparent.

◆ Encapsulate the item in a non-PVC plastic sleeve (Mylar is ideal). Encapsulation will not prevent the item from continuing to deteriorate but will prevent damage to the scrapbook page. A transparent glassine envelope provides similar protection.

◆ Photocopy the item onto acid-free paper. You lose the immediacy and charm of having the contemporaneous clipping, perhaps, but you retain the visual impact and have less of a problem with crumbling.

◆ Mount the item on buffered paper. Because of their higher pH, buffered sheets have an alkaline reserve and theoretically take longer to be compromised by acid migration.

It is also important to protect the book itself from dust, sunlight, humidity, and extreme fluctuations of temperature. Attics, garages, and basements are notoriously poor places to store paper-based things that you care about. In addition, it's best to store volumes upright, not weighed down flat under a crushing stack of other books. Handle the book gently, of course, and with clean hands. Professionals in the book conservation field handle materials with white cotton gloves and tweezers to prevent contamination from dirt or oils that might be on their hands, but this is a bit extreme for most hobby scrapbookers!

MOUNTING CHOICES

There are various ways to mount photos and memorabilia. If your album contains slip-in photo pockets, you won't need to worry about mounting. Otherwise, choices include adhesives and mounting devices such as mounting squares and photo corners. You can also cut small slits in the page with a craft knife and insert the corners of the souvenir into the slits.

Photo corners, which fell out of favor with the advent of magnetic-page albums, are very much back in vogue, now that it has been discovered that the PVC-laced self-sticking pages of decades past are actually harmful to photos. Photo corners are small, gummed V-shaped pockets that fit over the corners of the photos. The corners stick to the page; the photo itself never comes in contact with adhesive and can be removed easily from the page. Old-fashioned photo corners came in basic black, white, and silver; they were designed mostly for function and minimal visual intrusion on the album page. In addition to traditional lick-and-stick corners you'll now find convenient rolls of self-sticking corners in a variety of colors, as well as transparent ones. You can even play up the photo corner as a design element in your album by choosing corners printed with whimsical motifs or cut in interesting shapes like that of Victorian lace.

Other options include photo hinges, similar to the hinges traditionally used in postage-stamp albums; double-stick mounting squares; and individual photo pockets with adhesive backing that can be mounted onto a paper album page.

Some items are best kept in glassine or paper envelopes. Envelopes can be tucked into album page pockets, stitched to the page with cotton thread, or hole-punched and inserted into a ring binder. Also available are gummed, prepunched strips to attach to an envelope or page so it can be fastened into a ring binder.

with the grain

If you are making a scrapbook from scratch, bookbinders say that the "grain" of the paper and cover boards is very important, as is the grain of any fabric you might use. The grain of paper or board is just like the grain of wood and fabric. Always work with the grain running parallel to the spine of the book. This will help the cover and pages to stay flat and to open easily without tearing or being otherwise damaged over time. You can tell the grain of paper and cover board by flexing it. It will flex more easily with the grain. Paper also tears in a straighter line with the grain. The grain of fabric runs with the selvage edge. Ask for grain direction when buying paper and boards at craft or art supply stores.

Glue's Clues

Before choosing an adhesive, read the label carefully, especially if you will be working around children: Some adhesives emit harmful fumes. In addition, make sure the product is recommended for the material you wish to use it on. Use acid-free adhesives if you're going the acid-free route. You'll also need to decide between a glue that is permanent, which will hold items very securely, or one that is repositionable, which lets you experiment with the layout on the page. Some glues are two-way—they can give either a permanent or a temporary bond, depending on the application method. Choices include:

◆ Spray-mount adhesives—Spray cans quickly deliver a light, even coating of adhesive without the need to apply a lot of pressure to the item being glued. For best coverage, spray the glue in a cross-hatch pattern.

◆ Glue sticks—These lipstick-style tubes, super-simple to use, minimize mess and are great for children's art projects.

◆ Craft (liquid) glue—There are many all-purpose glues available. For most projects, you'll want to choose a glue that will dry clear. Glues that have color when wet but dry clear allow you to see what you're doing.

◆ Fabric glue—This nonstaining formula bonds and dries quickly, making it ideal for all types of fabric applications.

◆ Tacky glue—Think of this as thick craft glue, good for bonding items heavier than paper; its viscosity keeps items from sliding out of position while the glue is drying.

◆ Glue pens—A rolling ball fitted into the narrow tip delivers glue in much the same way as a ball-point pen delivers ink. The pens allow you to glue neatly in a very narrow spot.

◆ Glitter glue—Typically packaged in a tube with a narrow tip, glue glitter is easy to control, a neater improvement over loose sparkles that must be shaken over glue. It comes in many colors.

◆ Hot glue gun—This tool heats special glue sticks to a usable consistency in a very controllable method of application. A glue gun is good for affixing three-dimensional objects.

CUTTING TOOLS & ACCESSORIES

Whether for functional or decorative purposes, cutting tools are integral to the art of scrapbooking—from cutting paper for book pages to cropping photographs and creating borders.

Some useful scrapbooking tools and materials, clockwise from top: rotary blade cutter, clear ruler, and paper edgers—pinking, jigsaw, zipper, Victorian—from Fiskars; archival photo corners (white strip); gummed-edge photo corners; grommets; glue stick; 5/16-inch hole punch (purple handle). Underneath the scrapbook: two-sided craft mat; circle cutter. In the left basket: X-Acto knife; razor cutter; swivel cutter; glue pen; gold rolling ball pen; acid-free photo stick. In the front basket: rotary cutter disks; rotary blades.

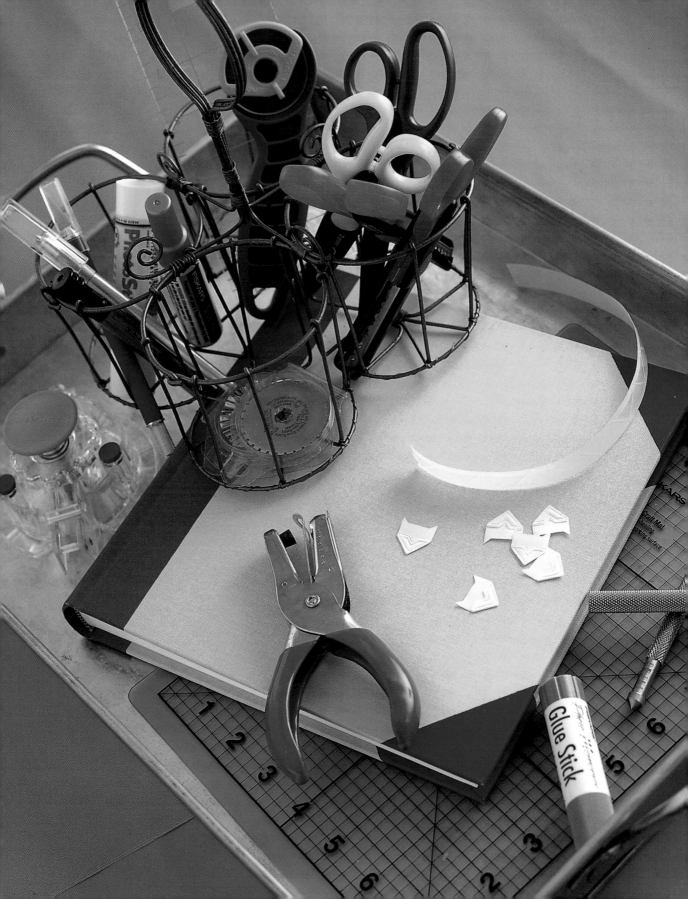

◆ Paper scissors—Invest in a couple of pairs of decent paper scissors. Long-bladed scissors make quick work of cutting out large, not-too-intricate shapes. Scissors with short, sharp, fine blades work well for cutting out small forms, such as a detail from a magazine picture or a family photograph.

◆ Fabric scissors—Purchase a good-quality pair of fabric shears and reserve them only for fabric because it is important to have sharp scissors to cut fabric cleanly.

◆ Pinking shears—Designed specifically for fabric, these give a decorative zigzag edge and prevent fraying.

◆ Special-edged scissors (paper edgers)— Once upon a time, pinking shears were about the fanciest scissors imaginable; today, they're tame amid scrapbooking scissors with elaborately curved or jagged blades shaped like bat wings, ocean waves, Gothic moldings, and so on. These decorative scissors quickly enliven a page border, photo mat, or other piece of paper memorabilia.

◆ Corner cutters—Scissors-style corner edgers and paper-punch–style corner rounders make it easy to transform an ordinary square corner into an edge that's curved or elegantly contoured, adding a subtle decorative element to a scrapbook page.

◆ X-Acto (craft) knife—In the days before desktop publishing, the craft knife was an indispensable graphic design tool, and it's still useful for hobbyists, primarily for cutting paper or other lightweight materials. An X-Acto knife is handy for quick small slices and also for intricate cutting that would be too cumbersome with ordinary scissors. It looks like a pen that's fitted with a small, thin, sharp blade. For best results, replace the blade as soon as it begins to get dull. Swivel-bladed versions facilitate the cutting of curves.

◆ Mat (utility) knife—Similar in function to an X-Acto knife, a mat knife or utility knife has a more robust handle and stronger blade (either a regular square-edge razor blade or pointed utility blade) that can slice through corrugated cardboard, foamboard, mat board, and more. For thicker materials, first score one side of the material, bend it backwards on the score line, then cut through the opposite side. Mat knives are handy if you are making a scrapbook from scratch.

◆ Rotary cutter—Think of this as a pizza cutter for paper or fabric that allows you to cut through several layers at once. A rotary cutter is useful when cutting paper to make pages for a scrapbook because it makes long, straight cuts and gives a cleaner edge than you might get with scissors, which sometimes leave little nicks or burrs. Also, it's faster and requires less hand strength and effort: You simply roll the rotary cutter over the paper and it's cut. Both straight and wavy cutting discs are available. The wavy-edged rotary cutter (think of a fluted pastry wheel) is useful for making cuts with decorative edges.

◆ Circle cutter—Bearing some kinship to an artist's (or mathematician's) compass, but fitted with a cutter instead of a pencil, the cutter adjusts to make circular cutouts of varying sizes. Circle cutters leave smooth edges free of the nicks that are almost inevitable with scissors. They facilitate cutting round shapes (such as photos and caption blocks) to add visual contrast to square items.

◆ Paper cutters—In addition to the heavy-duty, swing-arm paper cutters found in offices and schools, there are diminutive trimmers that are ideal for home use. Options include smaller versions of the swing-arm cutter as well as trimmers fitted with rotary blades or straight razors. Paper trimmers permit cutting of multiple sheets of paper at a time, and give a clean, professional-looking finish. The small ones are handy for cropping photos and other items.

◆ Cutting mat—When working with rotary cutters or knives, a cutting mat is essential to protect the table or counter underneath. Marked into measured grid squares, a ruled cutting mat also helps to keep fabric or paper square and properly measured.

◆ T-square—Another way to keep fabric or paper square for cutting is to use a metal or plastic graphic designer's T-square, a carpenter's square, or a heavy ruler.

JOURNALING TOOLS

The art of journaling—amplifying and explaining your memorabilia by writing captions or descriptions—is often a key to the charm and personality of handcrafted scrapbooks. Acid-free pens, markers, ink pads, and paints are available in a rainbow of colors, including metallics. Tips for pens and markers include ultra-fine point, for outlining and inking in fine detail; brush tips, which yield an effect similar to that of watercolors; squared-off or chisel tips, which work well for certain types of lettering; and calligraphy pens, with which you can improvise a credible imitation of calligraphy even if you have no formal training in the art.

EMBELLISHMENTS

There are many options for embellishing scrapbook pages:

◆ Stencils—Paper, plastic, and brass stencils designed specifically for memory books are available in countless designs, from whimsical teddy bears to various alphabet styles. Stencils intended for home decorating can likewise be useful. Use them with pens, markers, daubed paint, or embossing powder. A stenciled shape can add a single decorative element to a page, be used as a frame or background for a photo,

cloth for album covers

In general, woven fabrics will prove easier to work with than knits for covering an album. A few choices include:

- Bookbinding cloth— The choice of professional bookbinders, bookbinding cloth is designed to be applied with adhesive rather than needle and thread; available through bookbinding supply companies.

- Pinwale corduroy—Corduroy, like velvet, has a "nap," which is to say, the shade of the fabric looks different depending on the way it's held. In general, using corduroy with the nap so it brushes up will give the deepest, most lustrous effect.

- Muslin—Muslin is inexpensive and neutral, but its weave may get off-kilter; pull it tautly over the book from opposite corners to keep the grain of the fabric straight.

- Heavy moiré silk—This looks beautiful for a wedding album or other formal book. Be patient when you work with it; it can be very slippery.

- Denim—Inexpensive and fun to work with. Worn and lightweight denim will be easier to shape than stiff, heavy, unwashed denim.

- Cotton flannel—Soft and cuddly, flannel is just right for a baby book.

- Kettle cloth—This tightly woven but very flexible fabric comes in many printed patterns.

create a page border, or be repeated to give a common unifying "stamp" to several pages.

- Templates—Really a kind of stencil, there are templates available to create hand-drawn borders for photographs or pages or to provide patterns of straight lines for journaling.

- Rubber stamps—Stamps range from tiny shapes to page-size designs that will make a border around an entire page. Decorative alphabet stamps can be used as the starting point for headlines to introduce each scrapbook page.

- Hole punches—The utilitarian, hand-held single-hole squeeze punch from elementary school days has been considerably upgraded. Now, you can choose from fanciful punches that produce cutouts shaped like teddy bears, hearts, and more, as well as two- and three-hole punches and heavy-duty circle models that can punch through cardboard or multiple layers of paper. Lacking a heavy-duty punch, you can make holes in tough materials with an awl, chisel, or drill. You can also use a hammer and an awl-like tool called a drive punch or leather hole punch (available where bookbinding supplies are sold) to create holes in thick board and fabric.

- Stickers—Today, there are thousands of acid-free stickers in almost any motif or design. Like stencils and other icons, repeating stickers can bring a cohesive theme to a scrapbook.

- Die-cut paper shapes—Choose from solid-colored images stamped from paper for a subtle silhouette, or from elaborately printed forms. These can add a lively theme to your scrapbook page, or you can use them as templates to trace shapes onto paper.

◆ Sealing wax—In the days before digital encryption, an unbroken wax seal on an envelope signified the safe, private delivery of a letter. Today, sealing wax mainly has a decorative purpose and can be used to give scrapbook covers or labels a vintage appearance. Look in stationery stores for colored sticks of sealing wax, which resemble small, shiny, hard candles. The wax is melted and dripped onto paper, where you emboss a design into it with a metal sealing wax stamp while the wax is still soft.

◆ Ribbons—Grosgrain, velvet, or satin ribbons attached to the binding can serve as a built-in bookmark; or fasten ribbons to the front and back cover of a scrapbook to make a tie closure. Woven ribbon (see project, page 80) makes an attractive cover. Bits of ribbon can be formed into decorative bows or rosettes; wire-edged ribbon works well for larger flower decorations.

◆ Lace—An eyelet lace border can give a country flourish to a gingham scrapbook cover; fancier lace works nicely on a more formal book. Try sewing an antique doily or linen handkerchief to a scrapbook cover.

Fabrics and Trims

Concealed behind a custom-made fabric cover, a plain-Jane notebook becomes a Cinderella. In general, choose a medium-weight fabric that will be substantial enough to stay in place on the cover without wiggling, unraveling, or ripping from handling; but, at the same time, the fabric should be light enough so that turning under the raw edges won't make the book unnecessarily bulky. To prevent the

embellishing fabric covers

If you choose fabric to decorate your album, you can personalize it even further with these additions:

◆ Decorate the cover with buttons, beads, or sequins.

◆ Piece together a miniature quilt or appliquéd picture for the cover.

◆ Using fabric underneath as a base, fashion a woven cover from grosgrain (or another ribbon with good body) or from strips of fabric with the raw edges turned under.

◆ Sew pockets onto the front and back (or use a section of blue jeans with a pocket) to hold small treasures related to the scrapbook's theme: a set of keys, a string of beads, travel souvenirs, a baby rattle or booties, a small toy, or seashells.

raveling of loosely woven edges, cut the fabric with pinking shears or strengthen the edges with a commercial "no fray" product (available at craft stores).

STORAGE SOLUTIONS

Perhaps you have memorabilia that you would like to display and store in something other than a scrapbook. In fact, for three-dimensional keepsakes, you'll need three-dimensional storage (see page 67 for some ideas). An old shoe box is traditional; craft stores and photo-supply shops offer acid-free shoe box–sized boxes (and other sizes) designed for storing photos and negatives. These can be transformed into memory boxes—the box itself becoming a work of art that encourages people to peek inside (see projects, pages 64 and 88).

Scrapbookers dedicated to acid-free work even keep their supplies and tools organized in special acid-free drawers, boxes, and containers. Often, they use special albums for small bits (photo corners, stickers, die-cuts) so items are separated, unwrinkled, and visible at a glance.

CYBER SCRAPBOOKS

The home computer revolution has opened a world of possibilities for scrapbookers. The computer can be a tool for conventional scrapbooking—you can print page layouts, photo borders, and captions to mount in your regular album—or you can go completely cyber and create and store the scrapbook in digital form from start to finish. With your computer, you can design, manipulate, store, and print scrapbook/photo album pages; you can even e-mail family history pages to your cousin in Seattle.

◆ Digital cameras—Unlike a conventional camera, which records an image on film that can be used just once, a digital camera captures the image on a disk that can be used over and over. With a conventional camera, you may wait a week to have film developed, only to discover that there's not one decent shot of the birthday girl. With a digital camera, you view the image immediately in the camera itself, just as you review videotape with a videocamera. If you're not happy with the shot, you can record over it right away. If you like the picture, load it directly into your computer. From there, print it out exactly as it was shot, or you can manipulate the image in any number of ways: altering the crop, changing colors of background and clothing, retouching faces. If you use a graphic design software program, you can create composite photos: Imagine, a photo that shows a virtual family reunion, with all the far-flung relatives together in one digital place!

Even if you don't have a digital camera, you can still take advantage of computerized photography. Many commercial developers will return photos in disk form to you; you may even have the option of having the developed photos "delivered" to you via e-mail.

◆ Scanners—With an electronic scanner you can convert an image—photograph or document—into code that your computer stores and then translates into a complex pattern of dots to recreate on your screen, upload onto the Internet, or print out. The quality of the resulting picture relates to the dpi (dots per inch); the higher the dpi, the better the image. A dpi of 150 will usually give you a good reproduction of an image.

For cyber scrapbookers, the scanner is a great way to store and preserve vintage family photos as well as miscellaneous images—children's drawings, for example. You can also manipulate a scanned image as you'd like, such as lightening its colors or cropping it.

Page Layouts

Once photos or documents are loaded onto your computer, you can use a page layout software program to design your pages. You'll probably want software designed for home/family use rather than for professional graphic designers; the software costs much less and is likely to be more user-friendly. Most software does everything you would do in designing a scrapbook page by hand (positions photos, typesets and places captions, embellishes a page with borders or clip art)

and it gives you access to special effects such as shadows, reverse images, and photo manipulation. See how you'd look as a blonde, or how your living room would look with pink walls instead of white.

adapting projects

The projects you will find in Chapter Two cover a range of themes and techniques, most of which can be undertaken by a beginner. For many of the projects, especially those created from scratch with bookbinding techniques, we provide fairly specific measurements; keep in mind that these measurements can be changed as long as the elements of the scrapbook remain in proportion to one another.

If you'd like to personalize a store-bought album, see the projects on pages 39, 60, 77, 80, and 105; if you prefer to create an album from scratch, refer to pages 35, 45, 49, 68, 73, 84, 92, and 101 for project ideas. It is also possible to display and store important memorabilia in a memory box or shadow box, and for these projects, refer to pages 53, 64, and 88.

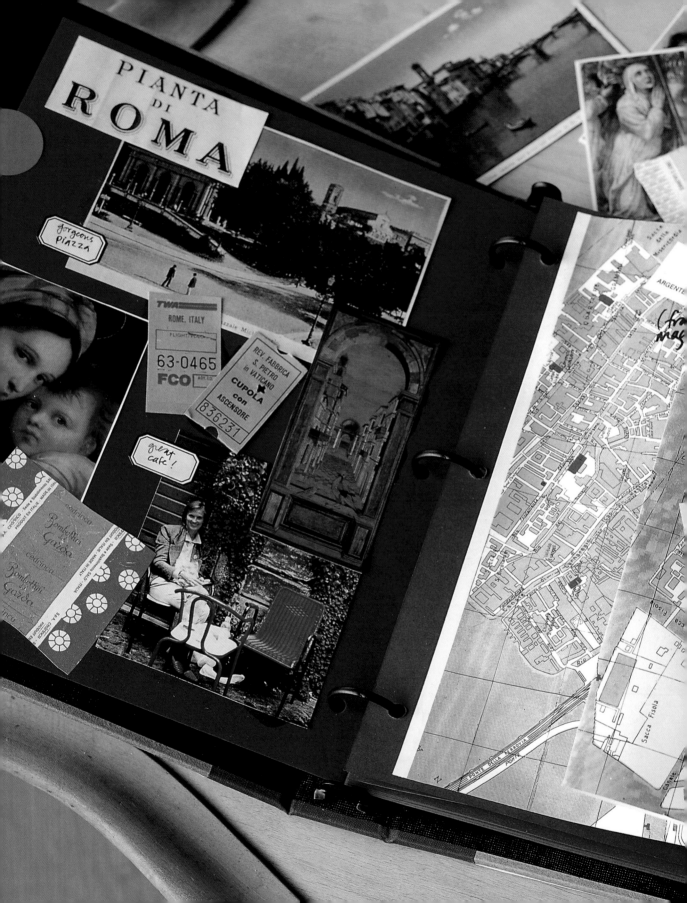

A collage of travel memorabilia will bring back all the richness of a vacation. Quite often it is the ephemera of everyday life that adds a richness to photographs, postcards, and other conventional travel souvenirs. A map has been marked with places visited, and is supplemented by ticket stubs from museums and various means of transportation, postcards, snippets of brochures, and photographs to create a many-layered scrapbook page.

chapter two

the art of scrapbooking

There are as many reasons for making a scrapbook as there are styles of scrapbooks. Weddings, babies, and milestone birthdays traditionally spark lots of photo-taking and reflection; in this chapter, we've included projects for preserving these most special memories. But everyday moments have their beauty and importance in the warp and woof of a lifetime's fabric, and you'll find ideas for recording these, too. Here, we've created 16 totally new memory books and keepsake boxes, along with step-by-step instructions so you can duplicate the projects at home. Some begin with purchased albums, which we personalize to suit a chosen theme; others are started from scratch. Some of these projects introduce basic bookbinding techniques, which can be adapted for many kinds of albums.

Consider these scrapbooks, albums, journals, and memory boxes as inspiration, to be adapted for any theme. With a change of materials or palette, a baby book can become an anniversary book, a gardener's workbook can become a decorator's journal. The only limit is your imagination.

design

Just as music is sound and silence, so graphic design (the way a page is set up) depends on the balance and interaction of words, images, and blank space. There are no rules when you're creating a scrapbook or photo album page layout; the result must only be pleasing to the eye—your eye. That said, a few considerations will help you to decide just how to achieve an effective page layout.

Old-fashioned photo albums had page after page of photos mounted squarely in unwavering rows. You will add visual interest and make information easy to grasp in your scrapbooks by varying photo placement, adding captions, and embellishing the pages.

Before you begin, flip through a few magazines or illustrated books and take a closer look at pages that appeal to you as well as those you don't really care for. Is your eye drawn first to the pictures or to the words? Is the type size and style readable? Do elements compete with each other for your attention? Does the page look "clean" (easy to understand at a glance) or is it just plain boring? Is the layout too cluttered to lead you through in an orderly way? Or is it a clever balance that lets you readily catch on to the main idea, but also reveals more subtle details each time you study it anew?

Start with just a few elements on your scrapbook page and build gradually. Keeping things simple to begin with helps you focus on the layout and what is important. Once the essentials are in place, add layers carefully and one at a time, always being careful not to let the page become too cluttered. In most cases, think about the positioning of each element so that you end up with an attractive, clear composition that looks well-planned and executed, rather than just a conglomeration of items pasted hodge-podge around the page. Try laying out the sequence of pictures and elements first before fixing them permanently in position, and adjust the sequence and organization until you are happy with it.

Ask yourself, "What's the focal point of the page?" Think about the feeling you wish to convey or the image you want to feature, and position objects so that the eye is naturally drawn toward the most important element.

Strive for balance between the starring and supporting elements. For a page in a wedding memory book, for example, you may have a closeup of the bride and groom cutting the cake. A simple caption underneath might enhance the story, while a headline in 3-inch-high letters of gaudy red glitter will almost certainly detract from the photo. On the other

Graphic designers use many techniques to subtly enhance a page. Consider the following:

- Don't feel you have to fill in every last bit of the page. A bit of white space can give a page a bit of breathing room. Try to edit the selections for each page ruthlessly!

- Variety is important in layout and type. Contrast size, style, or color of typeface for headings and captions, but try not to change typefaces or sizes too often.

- Focus on the important elements first and build the layout around them. Make sure it's obvious which caption goes with which photo.

- Add layers gradually. Put captions or little bits of text into boxes with a tinted background (like this one), for example. In a photo album, you could match the color of a border or frame for a photo and the background for a caption.

- Consider facing pages in relation to each other. Is each page self-contained, or does it become a "spread"? If it's a spread, consider how to link the two pages for good flow, such as having a headline span both pages or framing the outer edges of the pages with a continuous border.

- If most of the items on a page are lined up square, give emphasis to a special item by mounting it at an angle.

hand, a glittery gold border around a photo of a high school play might suggest a theater marquee. It all depends on content and context.

Balance and positioning also come into play when you think about the visual "weight" of the elements on the page. A large, dark picture mounted at the top of a page might look top-heavy, especially if it appears to be squishing a tiny caption below. Crowding lots of images, even at angles, on a page will convey a frenetic "day in the life" of a toddler, but might be inappropriate for a more formal subject.

Consider perspective. Where is the viewer in relation to the subject? Looking down at someone from a high vantage point? Eye-to-eye? Looking up? Perhaps other elements on the page can be positioned to lead the eye naturally to the main area of interest.

Variety keeps a page (or a series of pages) lively. Don't feel that all photos on the page have to have a uniformity of focus; it's fine to combine close-ups and panoramas, or color and black-and-white images. Surround a big photo with lots of little satellite photos; inset or mortise a small interesting shot into a larger image with a boring or blank background.

While variety can sustain interest in a series of pages, a common element—a stripe of color on the edge of each page or a simple border—can provide a feel of continuity. You could also color-code pages by season or by topic.

photography

While depicting images of daily life and the surrounding natural world dates back to cave paintings, photography is a relatively new technique. Its earliest version, the daguerreotype, was introduced in 1839. The art has come a long way since then, with today's digital photography holding still-untapped potential for changing the way we record, store, and display images from our lives.

VINTAGE PHOTOS

If you're the family archivist, it's best to get old photos out of haphazard shoe box filing systems and mount them in photo-safe albums to protect them from light and dust.

Both black-and-white and color images degrade over time, although the silver-metallic process used to reproduce black-and-white prints is inherently more stable than the dyes that go into color papers and film. In addition, the color dyes (which are layered in the color print) deteriorate independently of each other. The blue layer in color paper breaks down most quickly, for example, so old snapshots may take on a somewhat sickly pinkish tinge.

If you come across vintage photos that are a little worse for wear, or family photos that you would like to share with relatives (but don't have the negative), a photo shop that specializes in restoration can help. Traditional photo restorers can create a new negative of a vintage image by rephotographing the original; and they can airbrush or retouch the photo if necessary to remove scratches or fold marks, redefine faded areas, or lighten shadows. Many people choose to retain some minor imperfections, however, feeling they add to the vintage character.

More and more restorations are now done digitally instead of using airbrush techniques. The image is scanned into a computer and manipulated to enhance contrast and sharpness and rebuild missing parts of the image. As in traditional restoration, if your photo has imperfections such as wrinkles, creases, or tears, you can have them removed in the restored image. Obviously, the more the photo is manipulated, the more time is required, and the more it will cost.

When comparing the cost of conventional versus digital reproduction, consider longevity, too. Digital photography has not been around long enough for anyone to know definitively, but black-and-white hand-printed photos will probably last 70 to 80 years, perhaps twice as long as the estimated natural life span of color or digital photos.

sepia prints

Many people enjoy the warm, amber colors of sepia prints. Sepia toning can be done in two basic ways.

- The traditional method can only be done with black-and-white photos. It consists of a separate chemical toning process on the black-and-white print itself. This method can double the price of the print, but done properly, the sepia toning actually serves as a preservative; a properly done sepia tone photo can last for 100 years.

- Another common method involves making a color photograph or color digital print, then removing the color and replacing it with sepia coloring. The expected life span of this type of sepia print would be roughly equivalent to that of any color print, which is to say perhaps 40 years.

hand-tinted photos

In the days before color photography became the province of every family shutterbug, formal portraits were always black and white, sometimes embellished with hand-tinting, a process in which an artist applies colored pencil or dye directly to the printed photo. In some cases, the hand-tinted color has outlasted the actual photographed image, a kind of ghostly commentary on the ephemeral beauty of art and life. Today, hand-tinting is an artistic choice. Some photo shops can do it for you, or you can purchase supplies and try your own hand at it.

Turn-of-the-century photos aren't the only ones that may need attention. Magnetic photo albums, with their "protective" plastic coating on self-sticking pages, initially seemed like they offered timesaving relief. Unfortunately, the adhesive and PVCs in the plastic actually hasten photographic deterioration. If you have a shelf full of these albums, you'd be well advised to transfer the photos to new photo-safe albums, or even make entire new sets of prints if you still have the negatives.

JUDICIOUS JOURNALING

Captions count! Sure, *you* know the people, but think about your grandchildren, or great-grandchildren. It's frustrating to inherit a box of wonderful old photos and not know if the subjects are your great-grandparents or the neighborhood fishmongers. At an absolute minimum, mark the photo envelopes with the date, the occasion, and the people included. Then, when you're ready to mount the photos in an album, you can get as detailed as you like in your journaling.

There's a pretty good case to be made, however, for journaling as you go to capture the immediacy and spontaneity of the experience. While the photographic image will not change, your emotional reaction to it will alter with the passage of time. Details of the day may well be forgotten. And while the photo gives visual information, it can't convey sounds, aromas, or flavors—but your journaling can.

For a more decorative look to your captions, try some of the following:

◆ Headlines/captions printed with rubber stamps

◆ Stickers or stencils

◆ Decorated letters, in the style of medieval illuminated manuscripts, or fanciful letters formed from animal shapes, polka dots, or flowers

◆ Headlines scripted in silver or gold ink (or white, for black pages)

◆ Press-type (transfer-type)

EDITING PHOTOGRAPHS

As with fish, not every photo turns out to be a keeper. Don't be afraid to edit your collection to weed out unflattering shots, fuzzy images, or thumb-obscured prints. Cropping (trimming) clearly focused but poorly composed shots can help keep an album interesting, too.

As you are laying out your pictures, keep in mind that if every picture tells a story, then a series of carefully chosen photos can relate volumes. The order in which your photos come off the roll of film is not necessarily the strongest way of arranging them in an album. By sorting through pictures from a birthday party, for instance, you may identify five or six really great shots of the birthday girl. If you mount just those images together on a page, the resulting layout may do a much better job of showing the story of the day than using every photograph. Save the other shots—of guests and party decorations—for a separate

photographing children

Photograph early in the day (or early in the get-together) before the child gets hungry, tired, cranky, overstimulated, or over-sugared. (Or, wait until the last moment for a truly "natural" shot!)

◆ Don't tower over a munchkin subject. Kneel or bend down and shoot at the child's level.

◆ Be casual. If you're down on the floor with the child, playing and talking, the child will relax from the wooden "cheese" shot and become more natural. Kids' expressions change all the time; keep looking through your viewfinder to snap the exact shot you want.

◆ Invest in a camera that will allow exposures in rapid succession to keep up with your little moving targets.

◆ Use fresh batteries to avoid missing a perfect shot because the flash didn't have enough time to recharge.

◆ Take plenty of shots to be sure of getting one or two that you really like.

page, or use cropped shots of special friends and relatives around the edges of the page.

PHOTOGRAPHIC SUCCESS

One of the best ways to guarantee that you will have photo albums and scrapbooks full of interesting images is to take the time to compose your shot, even if you're using a point-and-shoot camera. Some tips:

◆ Study the image in the viewfinder. Would it look better horizontally or vertically? Move around the subject to see if you can find a more interesting angle or way to frame the shot. Centering the subject is often not the most interesting composition. Sometimes you can use something in the foreground (a road or fence, for example) to naturally lead the eye to an off-center focal point.

◆ Study the background of the shot. Make sure there's not a tree or lampshade sprouting out of someone's head and that the subject will not be lost in a scene that's too cluttered or visually busy. Try to eliminate extraneous elements and simplify by moving closer or altering the camera angle.

◆ Timing is everything. Too often, family photographers interpret a guest's imminent departure as a signal to begin orchestrating complicated group photos. It's much better to take photos at the beginning of the party, while everyone is in an unhurried good mood,

with hair still combed and clothes still neat.

◆ Everyone agrees that photos of babies and toddlers with food smeared all over the face are adorable. The rest of the population will appreciate paparazzi who resist snapping shots of guests with full mouths.

◆ Become familiar with the range of your flash. Subjects beyond its range in a dimly lit room will look grainy and dark. Even though your eye perceives the subject clearly, the camera's "eye" is limited to seeing the area most brightly illuminated by the flash. Pose people three or four feet away from a wall so shadows created by the flash will "drop" to the floor instead of being reflected right onto the walls.

◆ Get in as close as possible to your subject to capture character and detail, especially if you're photographing flowers or other natural or small objects. But be aware, however, of the

crop tip

To experiment with cropping without making irreversible cuts to originals, make a frame from a piece of plain paper by cutting a window the size and shape of the crop you're considering. Set it over the photo. Even better, make color photocopies of your images so you can experiment with various cropped shapes and their actual position on the page.

limitations of your camera. Most point-and-shoot cameras lose focus when you get closer than about five or six feet to the subject.

◆ The photographic beauty of sunrise and sunset is well known. Early morning and late afternoon light have their own magical glow, too, while the even illumination of twilight around dusk is often considered the most flattering light of all by professionals. For outdoor photography in the glaring midday sun, try to use the flash as a filler to avoid harsh shadows on your subjects.

ORGANIZING PHOTOS

Most family photo albums are arranged in chronological order, but that's not the only choice. Other possibilities include creating a book about each family member (if you usually get double prints, you can keep a chronological "master" album and use the duplicates in smaller books); organizing a book of maternal or paternal relatives; or planning a theme book—a family birthday book or Christmas book, for example, or an album to showcase favorite activities such as volleyball games, beach outings, jam sessions, or other shared activities.

photographing in the rain

Don't let stereotypes get in the way of a "picture-perfect" day: A gray day has a soft loveliness all its own, with none of the glare or harsh shadows of sunny weather. Consider a rainy day in Paris in winter, for example. The famed gardens are dormant; trees are leafless; sidewalk cafés have pulled chairs and tables inside. Still, beauty lies at every turn. Soft, diffused light reveals colors and details—in the bright umbrellas of pedestrians, colors reflected on buildings, roads slick with rain, even in the shininess of wet street signs and glistening traffic lights.

So, dress for the weather, protect your camera in a plastic bag between shots, get a companion to shield you with an umbrella along the way, and shoot off a roll or two . . . then settle into a window seat at a cozy café, drink in the view while you warm up, and plan your next photographic foray.

photo album

This album, which introduces basic bookbinding techniques, calls for a bone folding tool (see page 84) as well as bookbinding board and fabric, available from bookbinding supply stores and some art supply shops (see Resources). Tightly woven bookbinding fabric has a backing so glue won't seep through. It holds in place nicely when glued to the board for a smooth, professional appearance. Substitute mat board and medium-weight fabric if desired.

1. Cut out the elements of the album: With the mat knife and ruler, cut two 8 1/2- by 12 1/4-inch cover boards from the bookbinding board. Lightly sand the edges. Cut one 3- by 12 1/4-inch hinge from the art paper. To cover the boards, cut one 22- by 13 3/4-inch piece of blue fabric and one 4 1/2- by 13 3/4-inch piece of contrasting fabric. For the end sheet, cut one 20- by 11 3/4-inch piece of blue fabric. For the pages, cut about 26 pieces of art paper, 9 1/4 by 12 inches, and the same number of spacer strips, 1 by 12 inches.

2. With the brush, apply glue to one side of a cover board. Carefully position the board on the wrong side of the large piece of fabric, leaving 3/4-inch margins on three sides. Apply glue to one side of the hinge piece and position on the fabric, 1/4 inch from the cover board. Apply glue to the second cover board and place 1/4 inch from the hinge, 3/4 inch from three sides.

3. To make a mitered corner, trim the corners of the fabric diagonally, to about 1/4 inch from the corners of the board. Apply glue to one long side of the fabric. Fold the fabric over the boards and the hinge and rub flat with the bone folder. Repeat on the other long side and then on the short sides.

4. Turn the book over. Apply glue to the wrong side of the contrasting

MATERIALS

large sheet (26 by 38 inches) 80-point bookbinding board

about 7 sheets (at least 19 by 25 inches) heavy-duty art or drawing paper, such as Mi Teintes from Canson

1 yard blue bookbinding fabric

1/2 yard bookbinding fabric in contrasting color or design

two 36-inch lengths 3/4-inch twill tape

TOOLS

mat knife

metal-edged ruler

fine sandpaper

brush

glue, such as Jade 403 or Sobo Premium Craft and Fabric Glue

bone folding tool

glue stick

hammer

3/16-inch drive punch

large darning needles

fabric and center on the spine, folding it over the top and bottom. Let dry. Apply glue to the wrong side of the fabric end sheet. Carefully position the end sheet on the inside cover, covering the raw edges of the cover fabric. Rub with the bone folder, pushing the fabric into the gully. Let dry.

5. With a few dabs of glue stick, attach one spacer strip to the edge of each page. Stack the pages together with the spacer edges all on one side. The stack should be about $1/2$ inch tall, measured at the spacer end. If it's not $1/2$ inch, add or remove pages and spacers.

6. Make a template with one more 1- by 12-inch spacer strip by punching two holes, centered and $1 1/2$ inches from each end. Stack four or five pages and mark holes on the top page with the template. With the hammer and drive punch, punch holes. Repeat for all the pages and spacers.

7. Fold the cover around the pages. Position the template along the spine edge of the front cover and mark two holes. Then reposition the template just to the right of where it was. Mark another pair of holes. Position the template along the right edge of the front cover. Mark a third pair of holes. Remove the pages. Punch holes (six in all) through the front cover with the drive punch, making sure you punch from the outside to the inside of the cover. Repeat with the back cover.

8. Assemble the book with the pages between the covers. Stick a pencil through the top spine hole. Thread the end of one length of tape through a darning needle. Thread the other end through another needle. Position the middle of the ribbon over the spine at the bottom hole. Thread one end front to back and the other end back to front. Pull tight. Thread the tape on the front through the hole to the right, to the inside of the cover. Then thread through the edge hole, inside to outside. Repeat with the tape at the back cover. Repeat with the second piece of tape on the top holes. Tie ribbon ends into bows at the edge.

❖   ❖   ❖

painted wood
photo album

Paint techniques used around the home, such as stenciling or sponging, can add a level of interest to a wooden or paper store-bought album or scrapbook. Here we have used a combing tool, available in craft stores and specialty paint stores, to create a textured, wood-grain look. Experiment with different effects by pulling the tool straight down or wiggling it gently along the way.

1. Remove the front and back covers of the album. (If the album comes with posts, discard them or use in another project.) With a rag, rub a base paint (we used yellow) onto the outside of the front and back covers. Wipe off the excess with a clean part of the rag. Let dry. Rub a contrasting paint (in this case red) on the inside of the covers. Wipe off the excess. Mix the third color of paint (in this case green) with the glazing medium, using equal parts paint and medium. With the foam brush, apply the glaze to the front of the cover. While the paint is still wet, drag the combing tool downward, creating a line design. Repeat with the glaze and comb on the back of the album.

2. Rub the base paint on the piece of balsa wood. Wipe off the excess. With the foam brush and various colors, paint the wood pieces. Let dry. Arrange the pieces on the balsa wood and glue into position with the wood glue. Glue the balsa piece to the front cover. With the small brush and the base paint, print "PHOTOGRAPHS" above the balsa piece. If you like, polish the entire surface with Butcher's wax to protect it.

3. Cut out about 10 pieces of black construction paper ½ inch smaller than the size of the album cover. Use the cover as a template to mark on one piece of paper where the holes should go. Punch the holes in the paper, a few sheets at a time. Reassemble the album with the paper, lacing the suede ties through the holes.

MATERIALS

unpainted hinged wooden photo album

acrylic paint in 4 colors

glazing medium

small piece balsa wood

small heart, circle, and leaf wooden shapes (available at craft stores)

Butcher's wax (optional)

3 large sheets (20 by 30 inches) black construction paper

red and brown suede ties

TOOLS

cotton rags

foam brush

combing tool

wood glue

small brush for lettering

hole punch

themes: family history

"Write what you know," teachers always instruct budding authors, and the same holds true for scrapbookers. Without a doubt, your own life is the most compelling story you know, and when you can fill in background anecdotes about your grandparents and previous generations, a family history scrapbook becomes an heirloom.

There's more than one closet in America hiding a shoe box or two that's brimming with deckle-edged black-and-white photos. Some of the subjects are smiling, others, somber; the outfits may include suspenders and spats, overalls and straw hats, flapper dresses or fedoras—but who are these people? Are they relatives? Friends? Total strangers?

If you've been faced with such a mysterious conglomeration of photographs, you already realize the value of labeling and organizing. Imposing order on the family archives may seem daunting, but with a little planning and some time, it is possible.

Begin by organizing and labeling the most recent photographs. Organize the packs of pictures into separate bags or boxes for each year, then subcategorize. If you're trying to catch up with the photos of several generations, you may find it easiest for now to organize the newest photos chronologically into simple books, with names, dates, and events noted briefly.

Identify as many of the people or locations in the photographs as you can. This is the time to enlist the help of older relatives who may recognize some of the people and provide details about birth and death dates, marriages, siblings and offspring, education, occupations, military service, hobbies, and family trivia that will prove useful as you research your family tree and go on to lay out the pages of your family history scrapbook.

SEARCHING FOR CLUES

Tracing your family tree can be a fascinating trip into the past, one that gives you a clearer understanding of how you arrived at where you are today and that also provides the pleasure of the hunt and the thrill of the find.

To begin, rough out the basics of your family tree, listing the names of your parents, their parents, and offspring, along with the date and place of birth, marriage, and death. When you've gleaned as much information as possible from relatives, family Bibles, and other sources you might have on hand, you should begin researching public archives.

Use each fact you learn as a springboard backwards. For instance, if your late grandfather is the last slot completed in your tree, and he was born in the United States, try to get his birth certificate from the local town hall or state archives; it will most likely list the names of his parents, along with their dates and places of birth. If you can obtain *their* birth certificates, you will have another link back in time.

Many amateur genealogists have found useful information from the Family History Library, created by the Church of Jesus Christ of Latter Day Saints (www.lds.org) in Salt Lake City, Utah. The Library, along with its national network of Family History Centers, has a vast compilation of genealogical records from around the world. You don't have to be a church member; anyone may use the service to access any of the millions of records (mostly on microfiche), the oldest of which date back to the 16th century.

Genealogical research can involve a tremendous amount of legwork, and there is still no true substitute for getting information straight from the original source:

◆ Visit your ancestor's birthplace or town of last residence. By combing through records at town halls, state archives, or county courthouses, you may find pertinent birth, marriage, and death certificates as well as property deeds and tax records, especially if you have an approximate idea of the decade to search. Older volumes are often handwritten but are typically indexed. It can be like looking for a needle in a haystack, but if you are patient and methodical you may well turn up a document that fills in one more piece of the family puzzle.

◆ Churches in the U.S. and abroad may have records of births, baptisms, and deaths as well as information about burial plots.

◆ Published indexes compiled by genealogical companies, as well as on-line indexes, may give clues to deciphering census data or passenger lists from ships carrying immigrants.

If your resources or time for travel are limited, you can gain useful information from the Internet. In some cases, a municipality, church, or other source of original records will post comprehensive records on-line; in other cases, an unofficial researcher who has preceded you may have transcribed and uploaded records. There are family history Web sites for some surnames, and you may be able to correspond with people—distant cousins, perhaps—who are researching the same surname. Simply call up your favorite Internet search engine, type in "genealogy," and you're on your way. Although you won't find every record for every location, available resources include records of births, deaths, marriages, census data, and property taxes.

LAYERS OF LIFE

A family history scrapbook can include photographs, of course, but you can add color and depth to the family story by including saved treasures, such as:

◆ Originals or copies of documents gleaned from genealogical research, such as birth certificates, marriage licenses, military records, property deeds, ships' passenger logs, and census information

◆ Newspaper clippings about relatives and family friends, including birth, wedding, and death announcements

◆ Letters, greeting cards, and postcards

◆ Family recipes and holiday menus

◆ Printed programs from recitals, graduations, and religious ceremonies

◆ Buttons or swatches of fabric from clothing (if the garment is still in regular use, you may be able to cut a snippet from a hem or seam)

◆ Report cards and diplomas

◆ Tickets from school plays and concerts

◆ Children's drawings, especially family portraits

◆ In the absence of actual memorabilia, especially of distant relatives, incorporate visual allusions to family members' occupations or interests instead. These could be contemporary vintage postcards of a relative's hometown, an image relating to an ancestor's occupation, or memorabilia of a favorite sports team.

MEMORABLE MEALS

Despite the time-pressed lives many of us lead, a good chunk of family life, from special occasions to ordinary weeknight meals, is still spent gathered around the table. Favorite recipes link generations and are sometimes integral threads in the fabric of family history. To help preserve these traditions, create a scrapbook/memory book of your family's favorite foods, including recipes. Now is the time to get Grandma to pass along the secret to her chocolate cake, or Great-Aunt Maria to finally write down the recipe for tortellini she learned from her mother.

Ask the cook some leading questions:

◆ Who taught you to cook?

◆ What were your mother's/grandmother's specialty dishes?

◆ What did your childhood kitchen look like?

◆ What chores did you have to do to get ready for holiday meals?

◆ What were your favorite dishes?

◆ Who did the baking? The carving?

◆ What tools did your mother have to work with?

◆ Where did your mother shop?

◆ What convenience products were available?

◆ What did you make from scratch?

◆ What was a typical table setting?

◆ Who was usually included at gatherings of the extended family?

◆ Do you have any funny stories about family meals?

Your family recipe book doesn't have to be a finite project; you can add it to continually. Include details of special-occasion fare and everyday dishes, and photographs of memorable meals; you can also include menus from dinner parties, perhaps even signed by your guests. If a family celebration takes place at a restaurant, by all means include that menu, too, as well as anecdotes about the gathering. This is a wonderful project to duplicate for holiday gifts. Ask the copy shop to fasten pages with a spiral binding so the book will lie flat when used.

REUNITED

Family reunions run the gamut from casual lunches or picnics with a few cousins to full-blown conventions with rented banquet halls and hundreds of guests. But whether your family's gathering is thrown together on the spur-of-the-moment or meticulously orchestrated a year or more in advance, it is a good pretext for creating a scrapbook. At the reunion, take photographs of different groupings of relatives (all the cousins in one shot, all the aunts in another) and take full advantage of the collective memories of the guests, especially the older ones. Assign one or more family "historians" to interview fam-

ily members, preferably on audio or videotape as well as pen and paper, about family lore and history, asking them in particular about their memories of relatives who have passed away.

As an end sheet to the scrapbook, create a family tree, affixing to the proper branch of the tree photocopies of baby pictures of each person, where possible; then adding beside the baby picture a photograph taken at the reunion. Or reproduce a map (local, national, or international as appropriate) marked to show how far afield the descendants of your common ancestor have roamed.

reunion program guide

It can be fun to devise a souvenir "program" booklet for reunion participants. Some ideas of things to include:

◆ A family tree

◆ Photocopies of family portraits

◆ A questionnaire to gather serious genealogical information for the family tree or to collect amusing anecdotes

◆ Names, addresses, phone numbers, birthdays, and e-mail addresses of reunionees

scrapbook I

A fairly easy bookbinding project, this scrapbook does not have spacers (see page 49), and so is best for displaying flat images. Its cover decoration—layers of paper topped by a family photograph—illustrates a nice way to embellish a store-bought album. If you have a steady hand, you can cut the scalloped edge for the cover picture frame with an ordinary pair of small, sharp scissors, but it's easier with decorative-edged scissors. Be sure to realign the blade carefully before each cut for a perfect, regular border.

1. Cut out the elements of the scrapbook: With the mat knife and ruler, cut two 14 1/2- by 11 1/2-inch pieces of mat board. Cut a 1-inch strip off the short side of each board, to create two 1- by 11 1/2-inch hinge strips and two 13 1/2- by 11 1/2-inch cover boards. To cover the boards, cut two 16 1/2- by 13 1/2-inch pieces of decorative paper. For the end sheets, cut two 13- by 11-inch pieces of contrasting paper. For the pages, cut about 20 pieces of natural paper, 13 by 11 inches.

2. Spray adhesive on the wrong side of one of the pieces of the decorative paper. Carefully position a cover board on top, leaving 1-inch margins on three sides, and a 2-inch margin on the fourth side. Position a hinge strip on this wide margin, about 1/8 inch from the cover board. Fold all four sides of the paper over the board and press to adhere. Repeat with the second cover board, hinge strip, and cover paper.

3. With a pin, mark holes all around three sides of the cover, 1 inch apart and 1/2 inch in from the edge, starting at the corners. With the hole punch, punch holes at the pin marks.

4. Starting at the top near the hinge, lace the 1/4-inch ribbon through the holes in a hemstitch. Then reverse hemstitch, creating a V-effect. Glue the ribbon ends to the inside of the cover.

MATERIALS

large sheet (at least 20 by 30 inches) mat board

large sheet (at least 20 by 30 inches) decorative paper

large sheet (at least 20 by 30 inches) contrasting decorative paper

about 20 sheets (at least 11 by 17 inches) medium-weight natural-fiber paper

5 yards 1/4-inch-wide ribbon

1 yard 3/4-inch-wide wire-edge ribbon

raffia

TOOLS

mat knife

metal-edged ruler

spray adhesive

small hole punch or awl

all-purpose white glue

scallop-edged scissors

5. Spray adhesive to the wrong side of one paper end sheet and carefully position on the inside of the front cover, covering the lacing holes and ribbon ends. Press to adhere. Repeat for the back cover.

6. Punch four holes in the hinge strip of the front cover, beginning 2 inches from the bottom and set about $5/8$ inch from the side edge and $5/8$ inch apart. Punch another set of four holes, starting 2 inches from the top. Use the cover as a guide to punch matching holes in the back hinge strip. Punch matching holes in the pages.

7. Assemble the book with the pages between the two covers. Cut the $3/4$-inch ribbon into four 10-inch lengths. Tie a knot at the end of one length of ribbon and lace through the top holes of the paper and cover, from back to front. Wrap around to the back and lace through the second hole, from back to front. Repeat with the second length of ribbon, going from the fourth hole to the third. Tie the ribbons together in the front in a knot. Repeat with the bottom set of holes and remaining ribbons.

8. To decorate the cover, glue a favorite photo or memento onto complementary papers trimmed with scallop scissors, and weave a raffia border. Glue to the front of the album.

❖ ❖ ❖

basic bookbinding terms

- **bookbinding board** heavy cardboard used to form book covers. Mat board can also be used to make the covers.

- **end sheets** the paper or fabric pasted onto the insides of the front and back covers of a hardcover book

- **fore edge** the side of the book that opens (in Western books, the right side)

- **hinge** the point where a cover opens. Hinges are created by attaching flexible strips of paper to the cover boards, or by cutting a narrow strip off the cover board and placing the strip about $1/8$ inch to the side. After the board is covered with fabric, this thin space creates a flexible joint.

- **spacers** narrow strips of paper placed between the pages at the spine to allow room for mounting pictures and other memorabilia on the pages

- **spine** the edge of the book where the pages are bound together (in Western books, the left side)

- **text pages** the pages between the covers. In scrapbooks, these pages are generally $1/4$ inch to $1/2$ inch smaller than the covers.

family history scrapbook II

Spacers—narrow strips of paper affixed to the edge of pages before they are bound into a book—serve to give books a little breathing room when photos and memorabilia are mounted. To reduce the bulk of this book, mount photos only on the right-hand pages; this also prevents photos from abrading each other.

1. Cut out the elements of the scrapbook: With the mat knife and ruler, cut two 14- by 9-inch cover boards from the bookbinding board. Lightly sand the edges. For the hinge strips, cut two 1- by 9-inch pieces oak tag. To cover the boards, cut two $18\frac{1}{2}$- by $10\frac{1}{2}$-inch pieces of fabric. For the end sheets, cut two $13\frac{1}{2}$- by $8\frac{3}{4}$-inch pieces of fabric. For the pages, cut about 30 pieces of art paper, $13\frac{1}{2}$ by $8\frac{3}{4}$ inches, and the same number of spacer strips, 1 by $8\frac{3}{4}$ inches.

2. With the brush, apply glue to one side of a cover board. Carefully position the board on the wrong side of a large piece of fabric, leaving $\frac{3}{4}$-inch margins on three sides and a $3\frac{3}{4}$-inch margin on the fourth side. Apply glue to one side of a hinge strip and position on the wide margin, $\frac{1}{4}$ inch from the cover board.

3. To make a mitered corner, trim the non-hinge corners of the fabric diagonally, to about $\frac{1}{4}$ inch from the corners of the board. On the hinge corners, cut a rectangle out of each of the two corners with the corners of the rectangles touching the corners of the board.

4. Apply glue to one long side of the fabric. Fold over the fabric. Press and rub with the bone folder to adhere. Repeat on the other long side and then on the non-hinge side. Apply glue to the fabric next to the hinge strip and fold the fabric over the hinge. The fabric should cover the hinge strip and overlap the board by about an inch.

MATERIALS

large sheet (26 by 38 inches) 80-point bookbinding board

oak tag or bristol board

1 yard bookbinding fabric

about 16 sheets (at least 19 by 25 inches) heavy-duty art or drawing paper, such as Mi Teintes from Canson

two 14-inch lengths $\frac{1}{2}$-inch-wide ribbon

two $\frac{1}{2}$-inch screw posts

TOOLS

mat knife

metal-edged ruler

fine sandpaper

brush

glue, such as Jade 403 or Sobo Premium Craft and Fabric Glue

bone folding tool

$\frac{1}{2}$-inch wood chisel

hammer

glue stick

$\frac{3}{16}$-inch drive punch

screwdriver

5. To make the slit for the ribbon: Turn the board over. In the center of the non-hinge edge, mark a ½-inch-long line, ¾ inch from the edge, with a pencil. Punch a ½-inch slit through the fabric and board along this line with the wood chisel and hammer. Thread one ribbon approximately 1 inch through the slit and glue the end to the inside cover.

6. Apply glue to the wrong side of one fabric end sheet. Carefully position the end sheet on the board, covering the raw edges of the cover fabric and ribbon end. Rub with the bone folder to adhere. (If the bone folder is leaving marks on the fabric, rub the fabric through a thin piece of paper.)

7. Repeat Steps 2 through 6 with the second cover board, hinge strip, cover, ribbon, and end sheet. Let dry.

8. With a few dabs of glue stick, attach a spacer strip to a short edge of each page. Stack the pages together with the spacer edges all on one side. The stack should be about ½ inch tall, measured at the spacer edge. If it's not ½ inch, add or remove pages and spacers.

9. Create a template with one more 1- by 8¾-inch spacer strip by using the drive punch to make a hole at each end, centered and about 1 inch from the end. Stack four or five pages and mark holes in the top page with the template. With the hammer and drive punch, punch two holes through the pages. Repeat for all the pages.

10. Fold the hinge of one cover to the inside. With the hole template lined up at the fold, mark holes on the folded hinge. Unfold the hinge and punch the holes (only through the hinge). Repeat with the other cover.

11. Assemble the book with the spacer side of the pages between the two covers. Put screw posts from the front through the holes. Attach the screw tops from the back and tighten with the screwdriver, if necessary.

12. Decorate the cover with ribbons, buttons, old photographs, or other family memorabilia.

❖   ❖   ❖

memory box

A shadow box is a wonderful way to display precious things that won't fit into a scrapbook. It's a form that lends itself to artistic creativity, as here, in the layering of eclectic objects and ephemera. The items chosen for this three-dimensional display reflect or allude to the personal interests of its recipient—a mom who ran a sewing business, loved to bake, doted on her small dog, had a closet full of shoes, and collected odds and ends. Some of the items were found in her home, others were bought at a craft shop and a dollhouse miniatures shop.

We used an old kitchen knife box, with slots at the top of the box to put the knife blades through, for this project. A wooden shadow box available from a craft store will also work well.

1. Unscrew the two screws at the bottom of the box. Remove the bottom piece of wood and slide the glass out. Lightly sand any imperfections or splinters on the inside and outside of the box. If you are using a purchased shadow box, follow the manufacturer's directions for removing the glass for painting and reassembling. Depending on your box's construction, you may have to replace the glass after painting, then arrange the displayed items before attaching the back.

2. Cover the work area with newspaper. Prop up the disassembled box pieces on inverted paper cups to keep them from sticking to the newspaper. With a brush, apply one coat of brown paint to the outer pieces of the box (that will not be covered with paper trim). This will be the color that shows through the cracks. Let dry thoroughly.

3. To create an aged look to the paint, apply the crackling medium to the box with a brush, covering all areas previously painted with brown paint. Let dry thoroughly. A hair dryer can be used to speed up the drying time of the paint and crackling medium.

MATERIALS

old kitchen knife box or wooden shadow box

dark brown and off-white acrylic paint

crackling medium

gloss polyurethane spray

heavy-duty all-purpose contact adhesive in a tube, such as Quick Grab

all-purpose craft glue, such as Aleene's Tacky Glue

picture hanger fasteners

TOOLS

fine sandpaper

glass cleaner

paintbrushes

foam core

4. With a large brush, using long, steady strokes, apply a coat of white paint to cover the areas painted with the crackling medium and brown paint. Try not to overlap the brush strokes, since this would cover the cracks that have just formed. Cracks in the paint will appear almost immediately. Let dry thoroughly, 24 to 48 hours.

5. Following the manufacturer's directions, spray the pieces of the box with the polyurethane spray. Cover with two coats, allowing to dry thoroughly.

6. Decorate the exterior of the box. We trimmed the front edges with a small measuring tape cut to fit the length of the opening and glued in place with the heavy-duty adhesive. The buttons and old printer's blocks spelling "MOM" were also glued with the adhesive.

7. The inside of this box was lined with dollhouse wallpaper. A pretty piece of wrapping paper or fabric could also be used. Measure the inside dimensions of the two sides and back of the shadow box. Cut the paper to fit. Dilute some craft glue with just enough water so it can be easily brushed. Apply a thin coat to the inside of the box. Carefully lay the cut paper onto the glue. Smooth the paper flat with the side of your hand, pushing any air bubbles to the edge of the paper. Let dry thoroughly. The flooring used in the box is a black-and-white checkerboard intended to be used in the floor of a dollhouse room. Measure the inside bottom of the box, and cut the flooring to fit. Glue in place.

8. Position the items inside the box in a pleasing fashion. It may help to glue small pieces of foam core behind objects that don't lie flat and are difficult to glue down, like our tin heart mold. The table, from an old doll's table, was cut in half to fit the box.

9. After everything is arranged to your satisfaction, begin gluing the pieces to the back. Use the craft glue for paper and lighter objects, and the heavy-duty adhesive for heavier objects. Allow to dry thoroughly.

10. Clean both sides of the glass with glass cleaner. Carefully slide the glass back into the slots, press the bottom of the frame back into place, and replace the screws that were originally removed. Screw the fasteners onto the back of the box for hanging.

❖   ❖   ❖

themes: children

Documenting the important moments in a child's life—from birth to first steps to first day of school to high-school graduation—can consume a hefty portion of a parent's life, not to mention a lot of film. Creating something with the photographs and mementos collected over the years is a lot more fun and meaningful than simply stashing them away in a box on a shelf.

BABY ON THE WAY

If you're expecting your first child, you're about to experience the world in an entirely different light. When you leave for that momentous trip to the hospital, pause and look back at your home, for it will never be the same again. Soon it will be filled with new sights and new sounds. The weeks before the new arrival makes an appearance are filled with anticipation and preparation, and although this can be a busy period, it is also an excellent time to create a memory book and make a record of "waiting for baby." The days of pregnancy can seem very long while you're in the midst of them, especially when you feel ungainly or out of sorts; in retrospect, however, you will look back at this time with wonder. In your memory book, you can include:

◆ Month-by-month (or week-by-week, as things progress) profile shots of the expanding belly, along with a record of waistline measurements (and weight, if you're not overly sensitive!). If Dad is experiencing a "sympathetic pregnancy," record his expanding waistline, too. Jot down any cravings.

◆ Your first baby's firsts: a description of the first time you hear your baby's heartbeat at the doctor's office; baby's first ultrasound portrait; a record of where you were when you felt baby's first kicks.

◆ Advice from friends and family members who are already parents. (Remember, you're not obliged to actually *take* their suggestions.)

◆ Predictions about the child's gender (also freely offered by friends and perfect strangers), based on the shape of your expanding belly or the way an object on a string moves in front of you.

◆ Baby shower photos and cards and records of gifts received. Include a couple of swatches of wrapping paper and ribbon.

◆ Lists of names you're considering.

◆ Photos and/or sketches along with written details of preparation at home, including notes about any furniture purchased or decorating for the nursery. It's fun to include swatches of wallpaper or curtain fabric or paint color cards.

This book's logical conclusion is newborn photos, but the story now really begins in earnest and can be charted in a Baby Book (page 60). Three-dimensional keepers—the newborn hat, outfit worn home from the hospital, unbelievably tiny diaper—belong in the Baby's Keepsake Box (page 64).

MEMORY BOOKS FOR KIDS

To a preschooler, a year is an eternity and all of memory stretches endlessly to fill a time that for the rest of us is speeding along perhaps a little too rapidly. While you will want to put away special photographs and memorabilia for the child to keep, there's something to be said for creating a variety of hands-on memory books specifically for the child to use now, over and over, to relive those precious times "when I was little." The books can build up a child's memory bank with details he or she will be able to summon up and remember with pleasure forever. If grandparents or other special people live far away, last summer's visit may fade from a youngster's memory. Keep the relationship fresh by making your child a book filled with photos of the faraway family members.

Coping Strategies

Grown-ups have their own self-help books full of tips for coping with almost any life situation that can arise. But some child psychologists believe that a custom-made book can also help a child cope with a potentially frightening experience. To calm fears about an impending hospital admission, for example, you can create a book with photos of the child and the hospital, along with a simple story line; be sure to include details that grown-ups might take for granted ("You'll change into special pajamas; Dr. Brown and her helpers will be wearing masks over their mouths and funny hats to keep everything nice and clean for

tough albums for rough handlers

Kids love looking at family photos, but large albums can be unwieldy. Make them their own albums with duplicate photos. A "brag book" size with sleeves to hold one photo per page works very well. You can also make your own album by affixing self-stick photo sleeves to cardboard pages. Punch holes in the pages and collect them all in a sturdy three-ring binder. Where practical, cover the whole page with clear, wipe-clean self-sticking paper.

you") and to keep the story line upbeat. The conclusion should always be something reassuring ("and then Mommy and Daddy will take you home"). Read the story often in the days leading up to the procedure.

A "what to expect" book can also go a long way toward sparking happy anticipation and smoothing the first day of nursery school or kindergarten. In advance, take photos of your child wearing his "first day of school" outfit, packing the lunchbox or backpack, and getting into the car or waiting at the bus stop. Again, include a reassuring wrap-up ("and at the end of your first day, Mommy will pick you up and we'll celebrate by stopping for an ice cream cone on the way home"). For a memory book, take pictures as the events unfold.

Saving School Treasures

Between the work children bring home from school or daycare and the masterpieces they create at home, paper and artwork can accumulate at an alarming rate. Encourage children to create their own scrapbooks and journals to record their activities and keep treasures, or as a permanent place for their artwork. Organize projects, worksheets, and grade-A tests in loose-leaf binders to help contain the clutter—and also to let children revisit and review the assignments. Containing

artwork, which comes in all kinds of shapes and sizes, is a bit trickier (see page 68 for one idea).

If your young artist agrees, use some of her oversize paintings to wrap gifts, a nice alternative to store-bought paper. Smaller drawings can become one-of-a-kind calendars or notecards (ideal for grandparents).

To save a budding Picasso's renderings, an artist's portfolio will serve for storage. You can buy portfolios made especially for kids or improvise your own: Punch holes along three sides of two large pieces of posterboard; then weave yarn, string, or ribbon in and out of the holes to lash the pieces together.

Another more durable way to showcase artwork is to glue it to cardboard or posterboard, punch holes in the boards, and then string the boards together with metal notebook rings, or install them in a binder.

A good permanent home for three-dimensional projects is a memory box, like the Baby's Keepsake Box on page 64.

Junior Scrapbookers

If your children are old enough to wield a glue stick and scissors, then they are ready to make scrapbooks of their own. Help them to plan thematic layouts for scrapbook pages, such as a garden of flowers or a school bus, then paste faces—cut from photos—into the flower centers or the windows of the bus. Fill in details with markers, stickers, and rubber stamps. Display pages in a scrapbook or on the wall, or simply collect them in a three-ring binder.

At My House

Children might not want to flip through the pages of an album looking at pictures of relatives. To give them a sense of family history, create a house in the spirit of the popular "lift-the-flap" books, where a young child can open the "windows" and "doors" to find favorite people. Here's how:

Cut a house shape from a large sheet of construction paper the same color as your house. Keep the shape simple (a child's square-topped-by-triangle-with-chimney rendition) or give a stylized approximation of your own house. Draw windows and doors, shutters, window boxes, and anything else you like. Cover the house with clear self-sticking paper. Cut out the windows and doors on three sides with a craft knife to create flaps that can be opened. To make shutter-style windows, cut the top and bottom of the window, then the center, to form a sideways "H." Securely tape a family photo under each flap, being sure to include at least one photo of each person who lives in the house—even the family pet! Glue the house to a sheet of posterboard or cardboard cut to fit.

editing junior's portfolio

You'd have to add an entire wing just to house the artwork brought home by some prolific pint-sized painters. Unless you have lots of storage (and only one child), you can't possibly save everything. Cull through the collection and preserve favorites in a large, flat box or artist's portfolio; store in a dry place. "Keepers" include:

- Firsts: the first time she prints her name; the first time he draws a face; the first time the face sprouts arms and legs

- Originals: works from the child's own imagination and scissors (as opposed to cookie-cutter projects pasted from teacher-cut shapes)

- Handcrafted cards for birthdays, Valentine's Day, and other special occasions, especially with messages for Mom and Dad

- Traditional "hand turkeys" and other pictures made with the child's hands, feet, or fingerprints

- Family portraits or self-portraits

If you still have much more than you can keep, consider videotaping images instead of keeping the actual artwork in every case.

baby book

A fabric cover is a colorful way to personalize a store-bought book. As a baby book, this makes a wonderful shower gift. The pink and blue scheme is traditional, but pastel green and yellow or even white and lavender would work, too. If the book will be a present for a baby who's already arrived, consider omitting the decorative shapes from one or two squares on the cover and instead embroidering the baby's name, birth date, and birth weight, or spell out the baby's name with felt cutouts.

1. To make the front cover, measure the width of the cover. Divide this number by 4 and add $1/2$ inch. Cut out eight squares of blue fabric and eight squares of pink fabric using this number as width and length. With a $1/4$-inch seam allowance, sew a pink and blue square together with the right sides together. Sew a pink square to the other side of the blue square, and a pink square next to that. Repeat to make four strips of four alternating squares. Sew the strips together, with the right sides together, making sure the squares form a checkerboard pattern and the seams match and are in line. Cut away the excess seam allowance and press open the seams.

2. Trace or sketch the eight "BABY BOOK" letters on the paper side of the fusible webbing. Roughly cut out and iron the webbing to the pink and blue felt scraps. Cut out the letters, remove the backing, and iron to the contrasting pink or blue squares of the front cover. Repeat with the star, heart, and flower designs.

3. Hand stitch around the letters and shapes, using contrasting thread for some of the shapes. Sew the buttons to the centers of the flowers and onto the empty squares.

4. To make the spine strip, cut a strip of blue felt that is $1/2$ inch wider than the spine of the book and as tall as the pieced-together front

MATERIALS

scrapbook with a width $1/2$ to 1 inch narrower than its height

pink cotton/linen fabric

blue cotton/linen fabric

paper-backed fusible webbing

scrap blue felt for letters, side scallops, and spine

scrap pink felt for letters

pink and blue fine embroidery thread

pink and blue buttons

24 inches pink satin ribbon

pink gingham fabric

FIRST BOOTIES

cover. To make the back cover: Cut out a square of pink fabric the same size as the pieced-together front cover.

5. Cut thin strips of scalloped felt the length of the spine piece. Sandwich one scallop strip in between the front of the book and the spine. Sew along the raw edge with a $1/4$-inch seam allowance. Repeat with the second scallop strip, back of the book, and spine. Cut two 12-inch lengths of ribbon. Cut four blue felt hearts. Trap one end of each piece of ribbon in between the two hearts and hand stitch in place.

6. To make the inside flaps, cut two pieces of pink fabric that are as tall as the pieced-together cover and 2 inches narrower than its width. Cut two pieces of pink fabric using these measurements. Sew a flap to the cover with the right sides together, $1/4$-inch seam allowance, and an end of ribbon trapped in between at the half point. Press open the seams. Repeat with the second flap, the back of book, and the second ribbon.

7. To make the edging of the book: Center the pieced-together front cover on the book. Measure the overage at the top and bottom. Multiply this number by 2 and add $1/2$ inch. Cut two strips of gingham, this measurement wide by the length of the combined measure of the front and back covers and flaps. With the right sides together, sew a strip to the top of the book cover and flaps with a $1/4$-inch seam allowance. Repeat for the bottom of the cover and flaps. Turn in the raw edge of the flap and sew a $1/4$-inch seam allowance. Fold the flaps into the covers, right sides together. Sew the top and bottom of the flap edges to the back and front cover pieces with a $1/4$-inch seam allowance.

8. To make the lining, cut out a piece of gingham that is $1/2$ inch taller than the cover and 2 inches wider than the distance between the flaps. Center the lining so it overlaps the flaps. With the right sides together, sew the top of the lining to the gingham strip at the top of the book. Turn the cover right side out. Fold in the raw bottom lining edge $1/4$ inch and press. Slip stitch to the inside of the book.

❖   ❖   ❖

baby's keepsake box

Keepsake boxes are like three-dimensional scrapbooks—places to store and preserve precious objects and sentimental items as well as photographs, letters, and other paper memorabilia. Use them to commemorate special events; or create a "time-capsule" box for a new baby, containing the front page of a newspaper, popular books, music, etc., of the day of birth. For this keepsake box, recycle a sturdy shoebox or purchase a new photo storage box from a stationery or crafts store. Line the box with wrapping paper left over from a baby shower, or fashion a collage from paper by making color photocopies of your favorite baby photos.

1. Using the box as a stencil, trace the shape of the bottom and sides on a piece of newspaper, adding 1 inch to the tops of the four sides (to fold into the box). Extend both ends of the two short sides out 2 inches, to create flaps that will fold around the corners of the box.

2. Use the newspaper pattern, X-Acto knife, and ruler to cut out a piece of fabric and a piece of fusible webbing. Iron the webbing to the wrong side of the fabric. Remove the backing. Carefully place the bottom of the box in position. Press with a hot iron to adhere. Bring up one short side and wrap its 2-inch flaps around the sides of the box. Press. Repeat with the opposite short side and its flaps. Bring up the two long sides and press. Fold the overhang to the inside and press at the upper inside of the box.

3. Remove the label from the cover of the box if there is one. Repeat Steps 1 and 2 to cover the box cover.

4. Again using the box as a stencil, make patterns to cover the inside of the box. On a piece of newspaper, trace along the bottom of the box, then cut out a pattern. Repeat with the four sides of the box, adding

MATERIALS

unpainted photo storage box

about 1 1/2 yards fabric to cover box

1 1/2 yards paper-backed fusible webbing

cardboard

decorative paper to line box

3 1/2 yards 1/2-inch-wide white grosgrain ribbon

metal label (if it doesn't come with the box)

TOOLS

X-Acto knife

metal-edge ruler

spray adhesive

fabric glue, such as Fabri-Tac

1-inch flaps to both sides of the two short ends. Use the patterns to cut out decorative paper for the base and four sides. Spray adhesive to the wrong side of the bottom piece and place in position. Repeat with the two short side pieces, pressing the flaps around the corners. Repeat with the remaining two side pieces.

5. Repeat Step 4 to line the inside of the cover.

6. To make compartments, measure the box to determine the length of the dividers. Cut out the cardboard to the same height as the sides and to the length desired. For each divider, cut out a piece of decorative paper the same size as the divider and a second piece 2 inches wider and longer. Spray adhesive on the wrong side of the larger piece and carefully position the divider on the paper, leaving a 1-inch border all around. To make a mitered corner, diagonally trim the corners of the paper, to about $1/4$ inch from the corner of the cardboard. Fold the paper over to the other side and press to adhere. Spray the remaining small piece of paper with adhesive and position on the uncovered side of the divider. Press to adhere. Repeat for all dividers. Glue dividers into position with the fabric glue.

7. Cut the ribbon in half. Center the ribbons on the base of the box, one at each side, and apply fabric glue to hold in place. Attach or reattach the metal label to the cover of the box.

❖   ❖   ❖

displaying 3-D memorabilia

Not everything you want to save fits neatly into a flat memory book. Three-dimensional memorabilia have a charm of their own, whether you have collected items of intrinsic and quantifiable monetary worth (children's toys, vintage dolls, antique silverware) or of simple sentimental value, such as seashells from a lifetime of beach vacations, primitive figurines whittled by your grandfather, or dozens of champagne corks.

Nowadays there is an abundance of shadow boxes, curio cabinets, and wooden display cases for sale. A glass front thwarts dust; a front-loading cabinet makes it easy to change displays. Creative collectors are used to improvising display cases. An old-fashioned printer's drawer, for example, has dozens of small compartments and can be mounted on the wall to make a lovely showcase for diminutive treasures such as miniature figurines, thimbles, or polished pebbles. Old kitchen or desk drawers can be adapted into shadow boxes. Wooden utensil trays (such as the one used in the Memory Box, page 53), either vintage or modern, can likewise become attractive wall displays, mounted either vertically or horizontally. For rustic curios— antique kitchen utensils, vintage seed packets, farmhouse artifacts—you can fashion an impromptu display case from a shallow wooden fruit box, such as the kind that are commonly used to package clementines or grapes for supermarket sale. Attach two eye hooks to the back of the box and twist a length of picture wire between them to form a hanger.

kid's art scrapbook

We've given this scrapbook cover album-style corners and used a colorful button as a decorative closure. You could adapt this for any kind of simple journal, perhaps a quilter's scrapbook or fisherman's log.

Inside, we use colorful envelopes instead of conventional pages as an easy way for kids to organize favorite art-class creations. It could also be used for birthday cards, trading cards, and more. If your youngster would prefer to display the memorabilia conventionally, fill the book with construction paper cut to size, instead of envelopes.

1. With the mat knife and ruler, cut two 14- by 11-inch pieces of mat board. Cut $1\frac{1}{2}$ inches off a short side of each board, to create two $1\frac{1}{2}$ by 11-inch hinge strips and two $12\frac{1}{2}$- by 11-inch cover boards. Cut two $1\frac{3}{4}$- by 11-inch joint strips from the black card stock.

2. Mark the positions for eight holes on one of the mat board hinge strips, starting $1\frac{1}{4}$ inches from the top, spaced evenly a scant $1\frac{1}{4}$ inches apart, down the middle of the strip, leaving about $1\frac{1}{4}$ inches at the bottom. Punch out the holes with the hole punch. Lay this strip on top of the other one and mark the holes in the same position. Punch the holes out of the second strip.

3. To decorate the covers: Use the sponge dipped in white paint to make a marbled effect on the front and back covers (like on a composition notebook).

4. To create the album-style corners, cut off at a diagonal the bottom (non-clasp) corners of four envelopes. On the wrong side of these triangles—the side with the folded seam—trim out the interior part of the triangles with scissors so that just a $\frac{1}{4}$ inch of the edge is left on that side. Apply glue to a corner of a scrapbook cover and slip a tri-

MATERIALS

large sheet (at least 20 by 30 inches) black mat board

sheet ($8\frac{1}{2}$ by 11 inches) black card stock

white acrylic paint

twelve 10- by 13-inch paper envelopes with metal clasp

shoelace

8-inch length black elastic

button

TOOLS

mat knife

metal-edged ruler

heavy-duty $\frac{1}{4}$-inch hole punch

small piece kitchen sponge (for painting)

acid-free craft glue

paintbrush

glue gun and sticks

angle, right side facing out, over the corner. Cut a new triangle from the envelope to fill in the space that you cut away, and attach it with glue to the cut-away corner on the inside of the cover. Repeat for all eight corners of the book.

5. To assemble the book: With the brush, apply glue to the long edges of one card stock joint, leaving a $^1/_4$-inch-wide strip at center free of glue. Press the joint to the underside of the front cover and its hinge strip, leaving a $^1/_4$-inch space between the cover and hinge strip. Repeat for the back cover.

6. Punch eight holes in the bottom (non-clasp) ends of each remaining (uncut) envelope to correspond with the eight holes in the hinges.

7. Assemble the book with the envelopes (clasp side up) between the two covers. Thread the shoelace through the top hole and tie a knot in it. Thread it in and out of the rest of holes (running stitch). Finish on the top side, tying another knot and trimming the end.

8. Punch a hole in the back cover, centered and about 1 $^1/_2$ inches from the edge. Fold the elastic in half, tie the two ends together, and thread it through the hole so the knot holds the loop in place on the inside. Hot glue the button to the same spot on the front cover.

9. If you wish, glue child's artwork onto a rectangle cut from one of the envelopes and glue to the front of the album.

❖   ❖   ❖

scrapbooking bee

Back in homesteading days, hardworking farm women welcomed the opportunity to attend quilting bees. In the "many hands, light work" spirit that also spurred barn-raisings, friends working together made short work of piecing bits of fabric into economical, useful, and ultimately beautiful creations of usable art. Quilting bees also contributed to the figurative fabric of the area, fostering a sense of community and giving women the chance to exchange family news, reminiscences, and homespun advice.

Today, telephone, television, radio, and a proliferation of publications—not to mention e-mail—make exchanging information easier than ever before. Still, nothing beats getting together in person with a group of friends interested in a common theme—other churchgoers, parents from school, "soccer moms," hobbyists, local historians. All around the country, scrapbookers meet regularly to swap layout ideas, information about sources for wonderful supplies, technique tips—and old-fashioned camaraderie. Groups range from impromptu get-togethers with just a couple of friends to highly organized conventions. You can even go on a scrapbookers' cruise!

CAMP
PINECREST
1999

NOTES

FLOWERS

kid's camp
journal

A clever alternative to the ordinary open-and-shut book, this accordion-style memory keeper works equally well as a freestanding display or portable scrapbook. Because it is so easy to make, it is a good journal for children, but it is also suitable for any occasion— to record impressions of an exhilarating hike or to give to Mother, with pressed flowers and pretty fabric snippets setting off literary quotes and remembrances from her children. The framed title page sets the tone—here, small seashells or smooth pebbles instead of twigs would also provide the flavor of carefree summer days.

1. With the X-Acto knife and ruler, cut a large strip of paper, about 7 by 36 inches. Fold the paper, accordion-style, every 6 inches.

2. To make the covers, with the mat knife, cut regular cardboard into two 7- by 6-inch pieces and cut the corrugated cardboard into two slightly larger pieces. Glue one corrugated piece to a regular piece, making sure the pieces are centered and the corrugation is facing out. Repeat with the remaining cardboard. Glue the covers to the first and last panels of the folded paper, with the corrugation facing out.

3. To make a tie, glue the raffia at the back center so that one end is long enough to wrap around the book and meet the other end at the side opening. Cover the spot where you've glued on the raffia with a small piece of paper, trimmed with the scallop scissors. Decorate the paper by gluing a dried leaf to the it.

4. Glue envelopes (to hold treasures), photos, dried flowers, and leaves to the pages. Print the title of the book on a small piece of natural paper with the rubber stamps. Glue twigs and pinecones around the paper and glue the paper to the front cover.

MATERIALS

large sheet (20- by 36-inch) natural-colored paper

regular cardboard

corrugated cardboard

45-inch length raffia

small gift-card or glassine envelopes

TOOLS

X-Acto knife

metal-edged ruler

mat knife

all-purpose white glue

scallop-edged scissors

ink pad and rubber stamp letters

❖   ❖   ❖

There's an old saw (so to speak) about how firewood warms you three times: once while you're chopping the trees, again when you split the logs, and finally, when they're burning in the hearth. Travel provokes a similar three-fold pleasure, from the excitement and anticipation of planning the adventure, to the joy of being on vacation, and finally, of course, the pleasure of remembering the experience.

To keep the good, the bad, and the funny vivid in your mind, take along a travel journal (an ordinary notebook will do) to jot down at least the bare bones of each day, even if you gave up daily diary writing back in sixth grade. At the very least, include the date and the place you stayed overnight, plus the weather and a list of the major attractions and restaurants visited. Even jotting down a short phrase or two that describes these places will help you later when you begin to write captions for your scrapbook. If you're traveling outside of the United States, make a note of the current exchange rate, any new foreign-language words or phrases you learn, as well as the local foods you try.

Say CHEESE!

Consider the following before you pack up your camera and film:

◆ If you purchase a new camera specifically for the trip, make sure you know how to load and operate it before you depart. Shoot off a couple of practice rolls at home to identify any problems with the equipment or your photo technique before you go.

◆ Most personal albums will be more interesting if you include pictures of yourself and your traveling companions. Enlist the concierge, a friendly waiter, or a shopkeeper to snap all of you together. Try to capture unique details of the trip in your photographs as well as the sights—the café where you had lunch is far more personal and can be more evocative than the Eiffel Tower.

◆ Label rolls of film and keep a small notebook to jot down at least cursory information about the photograph and its location. If you wish, write out numbers 1 though 24 or 36 (depending on the number of exposures on your roll of film) on several pages so it's easy to record the subject and location alongside of each exposure number. Otherwise, you may *feel* you're absorbing the area's history and ambience and almost passing for a local, only to return home and discover with dismay that one Roman ruin (or Irish castle or French church or Southwestern National Park landscape) has a distressing similarity to every other you captured on film.

◆ Film developing on home turf may be cheaper than in many foreign countries. Even so, it's not a bad idea to drop off a roll early in the vacation at a local film processor to make sure that the camera and film are working properly.

◆ If you're traveling within the United States, carry along film mailers and send each roll off to the developer as it's shot; you'll have a mailbox full of prints when you return home.

◆ If you are traveling with children, provide each with a disposable camera. These cameras take pretty decent photos and cost little more than a roll of film. You may be surprised to find that you have a budding Ansel Adams or Margaret Bourke-White in the back seat. In fact, it's not a bad idea to carry a couple of disposables for the grown-ups, too, for outings to the beach or to areas where you might not want to take an expensive camera.

◆ Upon returning home, label photos as soon as possible, before the glow of the trip fades and details begin to blur.

things to save along the way

A thoughtfully planned travel scrapbook can give pleasure long after the suitcases have been unpacked. Souvenirs to collect along the way include:

- Maps and itineraries

- A daily calendar of the trip, indicating location, weather, lodging, and sightseeing highlights

- Airline ticket receipts, boarding passes, rail passes

- Postcards, stamps, and travel brochures

- Ticket stubs from museums, national parks, campgrounds, theaters

- Foreign paper money and coins

- Subway or bus tickets and tokens

- Coasters or drink stirrers

- Restaurant menus, matchbooks, and receipts

- Stationery and other small complimentary hotel souvenirs (not the towels!)

- Seashells, pinecones, bits of driftwood, pretty pebbles, and a bit of beach sand in a sealed plastic bag

- Shopping bags or wrapping paper from stores

vacation scrapbook

Ring binders are probably the most versatile form of scrapbooks—pages can be removed, added, or reordered, and the binding accommodates bulkier items better than most books. Unfortunately, most ring binders look like office supplies (which they often are), so here we've dressed up the cover of one with a collage of mementos. A color photocopy of a collage would work, too; with this photocopy technique, you can also incorporate coins and other objects into the design that might otherwise be too heavy to glue to the cover itself.

Try dividing your book into sections by region or by experience (say, dining, theater, sights, or music). You may also want to make color photocopies of some of these items so you can cut them into smaller pieces. One page could be devoted to a map, with the places visited marked in red, and the actual map could be glued on the left-hand edge only so it can be unfolded. See the photograph on pages 24–25 for an interior shot of this scrapbook.

1. Measure the front cover of the binder. Cut the map to fit and glue to the cover. Make a collage by gluing other memorabilia (or color copies) over the map.

2. Make a tag for the cover by cutting out two rectangles of the black and white stock and gluing together. Punch a hole in the left side of the tag and tie a piece of white cotton twine through it as though it were a luggage tag. Glue the tag to the cover.

3. Make a section label with two dot labels by sticking one halfway on the edge of a page and a second dot on the other side of the page, sticky side meeting sticky side. Repeat every few pages as you fill up the album. Glue photos and memorabilia to pages.

❖ ❖ ❖

MATERIALS

hardcover 3-ring binder and acid-free 3-ring photo album pages

map or other large paper memento

sheet black card stock

sheet white card stock

white cotton twine

dot labels

TOOLS

acid-free glue

hole punch

themes: wedding

Looking back, many newlyweds report that while they can remember the hours of planning that led up to their wedding, the special day itself seems like a blur, remembered largely as emotions and sensory impressions. Actual details of the ceremony and the reception may be hazy; entire conversations can be forgotten altogether. Photographs help to bring back the details of the wedding, especially if you make sure to get more than the standard portraits. Ask your photographer to arrive early to capture some "behind the scenes" shots and encourage him or her to take spontaneous pictures of the event in addition to formal poses. Make sure you get shots of the setting, too, in addition to such details as the flowers at the ceremony, the bouquet, the buttons on your dress.

It is also fun to encourage guests to help capture candid moments. Leave one or more disposable cameras on each table at the reception, with a note requesting that guests each take a turn behind the shutter. If you wish, leave a notebook on each table (tie a pen to the book) and let guests record their observations and greetings for the bride and groom.

A Wedding Gift for Your Spouse

As a special wedding gift for your new mate, create a book filled with memories of your times together. If you wish, begin with childhood or baby pictures of each of you. The book can include photos of when you first met; menus from favorite restaurants; ticket stubs; the lyrics to "your" song; anecdotes; predictions or a wish list of where you hope your dreams will take the two of you in the years to come.

other wedding memorabilia

Round out wedding memories by saving items such as:

- An invitation and the guest list and seating chart (after all, didn't many hours of work go into finalizing these?)

- The printed program for the ceremony (plus handwritten notes from the planning stage), personalized wedding favors such as matchbooks, napkins, or table placecards

- Delivery memos and bills from the caterer, florist, formalwear shop, dressmaker, shoe store, etc.

- Pressed flowers from the bouquet and table centerpieces

- A swatch of fabric from the bridal party gowns; snippets of ribbon from the bouquets

Preserving Petals

Pressed flowers from your wedding bouquet or table centerpieces contribute their own beauty to your wedding memory book. For best results, choose small, flat-face flowers that will still show their character when pressed flat. You can purchase a flower press, or use the old-fashioned, low-tech method: Place the flowers to be preserved between two sheets of acid-free paper. (The acid-free paper helps with color retention, although blossoms will fade after a couple of years anyway. Even so, their delicate shapes can contribute to the beauty of the page.) Place the sheets between the pages of a large, heavy book and lay the book flat, weighted down by a couple of additional volumes. Don't limit your selection to the flowerheads; leaves and ferns can be quite beautiful when pressed, too. After about a week or two, the flowers should be pressed flat.

Mount the pressed flowers into your album with clear-drying acid-free glue, or encapsulate them in Mylar or clear plastic before attaching to the page. You'll likely need tweezers to handle the fragile blossoms. For fatter flowers such as roses that can't be pressed easily, press individual petals instead of the whole blossom. Pressed petals can look quite pretty as a border or embellishment for a memory book.

As an alternative to pressing, blossoms can be air-dried whole (remove leaves and hang the flowers upside down in a dark space for a couple of weeks), though the colors can brown considerably. For a more professional look, use silica gel to dry the blossoms at room temperature or in the microwave. (Silica gel is readily available at craft shops, specifically for the purpose of drying flowers.) Flowers dried with silica gel tend to retain better color and a bit more flexibility than their air-dried counterparts. Fill a container partway with the silica gel; lay the flowerheads upside down on the silica, then gently add more silica to cover. Come back in about a week, and your flower should be nicely dried.

If you give the container a quick zap in the microwave oven (typically anywhere from ten seconds to about a minute; exact timing depends upon size, number, density, and moisture content of flowers), the flowers will be dried even faster. A food dehydrator also does a nice job of drying flowers, and, like microwave-drying with silica gel, completes the process in a day instead of taking weeks, and also usually maintains color better than straight air-drying.

wedding album

Woven ribbon creates a beautiful cover for this store-bought album (we used a 10- by 10-inch album; if your album is a different size, you will need to adapt the measurements—cutting the ribbon longer or shorter as necessary and sizing the end sheets to fit). Grosgrain ribbon is easy to work with and gives a crisp, fresh look that is perfect for wedding photographs. If you have the ribbon from the bouquet, consider using it for the bow.

This type of woven cover adapts to other subjects. A family history, for example, could be done in rich dark-colored ribbons. For a record of a playing season, you could use the colors of a favorite sports team. Just make sure you choose ribbon that's fairly stiff: A ribbon with a lot of play will wiggle mercilessly as you try to attach it and is likely to throw off the "square" of the weave.

1. Cut the 1 1/2-inch ribbon into nine 12-inch strips and nine 14-inch strips. Place the 12-inch ribbons vertically on the cutting mat, positioning them close to each other. As you align each one, secure the top end with masking tape to hold it in place temporarily.

2. Weave each 14-inch ribbon into the 12-inch ribbons using an over and under technique, alternating each row. Continually check to make sure that the ribbons stay square. When complete, secure both ends of the 14-inch ribbons with tape. Check to make sure that the vertical and horizontal ribbons are square and butting up as tightly as possible. There should be no overlaps or spaces between the ribbons.

3. Take the album apart. On the front cover of the album, use a pencil to mark three holes 1 inch from the binding edge: one 2 1/4 inches from the top, one 2 1/4 inches from the bottom, and one in the center. Using the awl, make the holes in the cover. Make each hole large enough to snugly accept the 7/8-inch ribbon.

MATERIALS

10- by 10-inch (cover measure) plain photo album with screw fasteners

14 yards 1 1/2-inch-wide white grosgrain ribbon

1/2 yard white moiré fabric, 54 inches wide

large sheet (at least 20 by 30 inches) white light-gauge poster board or heavy paper

3 yards 7/8-inch-wide white grosgrain ribbon

TOOLS

ruled cutting mat

awl

spray adhesive

fabric glue

4. Center the front cover on the woven ribbons with an even overlap all the way around. If your album has fastening flaps—with holes that hold the fasteners—open it flat. Mark the position of the cover on the ribbons with a pencil. Remove the cover and spray it with adhesive. Reposition the sticky side onto the woven ribbon using the pencil marks as guide.

5. Beginning with the vertical ribbons, fold the ends onto the inside cover one-by-one, top to bottom, and secure using fabric glue. Secure the horizontal ribbons using the same process. Be sure to keep the ribbons straight.

6. Repeat Steps 1 through 5 for the back cover, omitting Step 3—there is no need for holes on the back cover.

7. Using the awl, carefully punch holes through the ribbon on the front cover to open the holes.

8. For the end sheets, cut the white moiré fabric into two 11-inch squares. Fold the edges in $3/4$ inch so that each square measures $9 1/2$ by $9 1/2$ inches. Press with a hot iron. Cut two $9 1/2$-inch squares of white poster board and fit one inside each piece of the folded moiré fabric.

9. If your album cover has fastening flaps on the inside, cut two $10 1/2$- by 4-inch strips of moiré fabric to cover them. Fold the edges of the fabric in $1/2$ inch and iron so that each piece measures $9 1/2$ by 3 inches. With the front cover face down, center the moiré strip over the flap so that a $1/4$-inch border is exposed on the top, bottom, and right side. Approximately 1 inch of fabric will be covering the flap; the remaining 2 inches of fabric will overlap onto the inside front cover. Glue the moiré strip to the flap and inside front cover with a thin layer of fabric glue. Repeat for the back inside flap.

10. Center and glue one moiré-covered panel to the inside cover, leaving a $1/4$-inch border all around. Repeat for the back cover.

11. Using the awl, open the three holes on the front cover, carefully going through the moiré-covered board. Also use the awl to open the holes on the front and back flaps for the fasteners.

12. Cut a piece of the $7/8$-inch ribbon 3 yards long. Fold the ribbon in half—to 54 inches—and from the inside front cover, thread the folded end through the center hole, leaving a loop on the outside cover.

13. Thread one end of the ribbon through a cover hole (going from the inside to the outside). Thread the other end through the other cover hole.

14. You will now have a ribbon loop in the center and two long strands of ribbon on the outside of the front cover. To make a bow, create a loop with one strand and thread it through the center loop. Take the other strand and do the same thing. Tighten the center loop by pulling it from the inside and adjusting the bow. The length of the final decorative ribbon is a personal choice.

15. Put the fasteners back through the holes in the flaps and add the photo pages. Screw the fasteners tight.

❖   ❖   ❖

wedding scrapbook

The crossed-ribbon binding of this scrapbook gives it an elegant finish. This binding style can also be used with other books, as long as the ribbon used is strong enough to hold the book together, yet thin enough to thread through a darning needle.

The bone folding tool called for here is a traditional bookbinder's tool, used for creasing paper and fabric or burnishing glued materials for a smooth, tight finish. It's a thin, flat tool that may have either a rounded or pointed tip. A clean wooden craft stick or tongue depressor can pinch-hit if you don't have a bone folder.

1. Cut out the elements of the scrapbook: With the mat knife and ruler, cut two 10 3/4- by 12 1/4-inch cover boards and two 1 1/4- by 12 1/4-inch hinge strips from the bookbinding board. Lightly sand the edges. To cover the boards, cut two 13 3/4-inch squares of fabric. For the end sheets, cut two 11 7/8-inch squares of fabric. For the pages, cut about 40 pieces of 12-inch square paper and the same number of spacer strips, 1 1/4 by 12 inches.

2. With the brush, apply glue to one side of a cover board. Carefully position the board on the wrong side of one piece of fabric, leaving 3/4-inch margins on three sides and a 2 1/4-inch margin on the fourth side. Apply glue to one side of a hinge strip and position on the wide margin, 1/4 inch from the cover board and 3/4 inch from the edge of the fabric.

3. To miter the corners, diagonally trim the corners of the fabric, to about 1/4 inch from the corners of the board. Apply glue to the top edge of the fabric. Fold the fabric over the board and hinge and rub with the bone folder. Repeat on the bottom edge and then on the sides.

4. Apply glue to the wrong side of one end sheet. Carefully position the

MATERIALS

1 large sheet (26 by 38 inches) 80-point bookbinding board

1 yard bookbinding fabric

20 sheets (20 by 26 inches) heavy-duty art or paper

3 yards 1/2-inch ribbon

decorative paper

TOOLS

mat knife

metal-edged ruler

fine sandpaper

brush

glue, such as Jade 403 or Sobo Premium Craft and Fabric Glue

bone folding tool

glue stick

3/16-inch drive punch and hammer

large darning needles

Mr. and Mrs. Richard Hamill Pew, Jr.
request the honour of your presence
at the marriage of their daughter
Allison Holt
to
Stuart Henry Meyler
Saturday the twentieth of September
nineteen hundred and ninety seven
twelve o'clock noon
St. Patrick's Church
Newcastle, Maine

Reception immediately following
at Grey Havens Inn
Georgetown, Maine

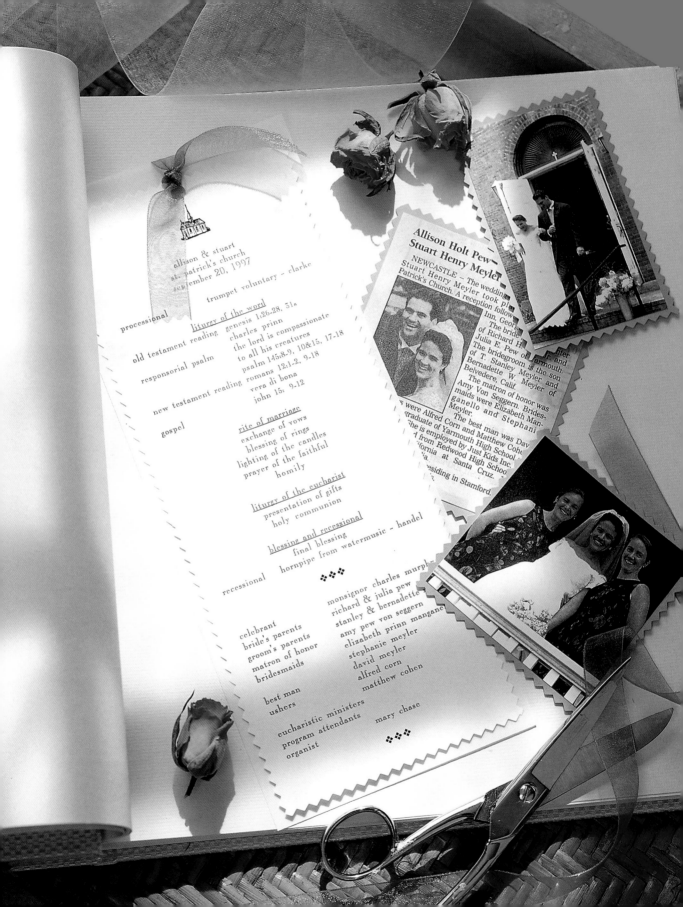

allison & stuart
st. patrick's church
september 20, 1997

processional   trumpet voluntary - clarke

liturgy of the word
old testament reading   genesis 1:26-28, 31a
                         charles prinn
                         the lord is compassionate
responsorial psalm   to all his creatures
                         psalm 145:8-9, 10&15, 17-18
new testament reading   romans 12:1-2, 9-18
                         vera di bona
                         john 15: 9-12
gospel

rite of marriage
exchange of vows
blessing of rings
lighting of the candles
prayer of the faithful
homily

liturgy of the eucharist
presentation of gifts
holy communion

blessing and recessional
final blessing
recessional   hornpipe from watermusic - handel

❖❖❖ ◆◆◆

celebrant   monsignor charles murph...
bride's parents   richard & julia pew
groom's parents   stanley & bernadette...
matron of honor   amy pew von seggern
bridesmaids   elizabeth prinn mangane...
                       stephanie meyler
                       david meyler
best man   alfred corn
ushers   matthew cohen

eucharistic ministers
program attendants   mary chase
organist

❖❖❖ ◆◆◆

Allison Holt Pew —
Stuart Henry Meyler

NEWCASTLE — The wedding...
Stuart Henry Meyler took pl...
Patrick's Church. A reception follow...
Inn, Georg...
The bride...
of Richard H...
Julia E. Pew of ...Yarmouth.
The bridegroom is the son...
of T. Stanley Meyler and
Bernadette W. Meyler of
Belvedere, Calif.
The matron of honor was
Amy Von Seggern. Brides-
maids were Elizabeth Man-
ganello and Stephani...
Meyler.
The best man was Dav...
...s were Alfred Corn and Matthew Cohe...
...graduate of Yarmouth High School...
...he is employed by Just Kids Inc.
...d from Redwood High Schoo...
...fornia at Santa Cruz.
...a.
...esiding in Stamford.

end sheet on the inside of the cover, covering the raw edges. Rub with the bone folder, pushing the fabric into the gully between the hinge and cover. Let dry.

5. Repeat Steps 2 through 4 with the second cover board, hinge strip, and fabric. Let dry.

6. With a few dabs of the glue stick, attach one spacer strip to the edge of each page. Stack the pages together with the spacer sides all on one side. The stack should be about ¾ inch high, measured at the spacer edge. If it's not ¾ inch, add or remove pages and spacers.

7. Make a template with one more 1 ¼- by 8 ¾-inch spacer strip by making one hole with the drive punch in the center, then two holes ¾ inch from each end, and two more holes exactly halfway between each end hole and center hole (five holes in all). Stack four or five pages and mark holes in the top page with the template. With the hammer and drive punch, punch holes through the pages. Repeat for all the pages.

8. Following the hole template, punch holes on the hinge part of the front cover, from the front to inside of the cover. Repeat with the back cover.

9. Assemble the book with the pages in place. Stick pencils in the top and middle holes to hold the album in position. Thread one end of the ribbon through a darning needle. Thread the other end through another needle. Position the middle of the ribbon over the spine at the bottom hole. Thread one end of the ribbon through the hole, front to back, and the other end, back to front. Pull tight and smooth the ribbon over the spine. Cross the ribbons and repeat through the next hole after removing the pencil. Repeat up to the top hole. Tie the ribbon at the spine in a knot, then a bow. Trim the ribbon ends. Glue a decorative paper frame to the front cover and glue an invitation in place.

❖   ❖   ❖

wedding box

Shelved on a bookcase, this memory box looks like any other volume. It's really a clever keepsake box to hold dried flowers, matchbooks, ribbons, and other wedding-day souvenirs, or any special memorabilia—letters from friends, or playbills and ticket stubs from theater outings. The instructions call for decoupage glue (see Resources), which works as both a glue and a finish.

1. With the brush, paint the outside of the box with one coat of primer. Apply one coat of decoupage glue to the spine, about 1 1/2 inches into the front and back covers, and to the corners of the covers. Cover these areas with tissue paper. Let dry. Add a second layer of tissue paper, if desired.

2. Apply decoupage glue to the front, back, and spine of box. Let dry. With the X-Acto knife and ruler, cut two pieces of decorative paper to fit the front and back covers, leaving about 1 inch from the spine edge and the two corners uncovered, and providing for 1/2-inch overhangs at the side, top, and bottom. Apply decoupage glue to the covers, spine, and inside edges, and carefully position the paper. Press to adhere.

3. Measure the top, bottom, and non-spine edges of the box and cut three pieces of ecru paper to fit. Apply decoupage glue to the edges and position the paper. Press to adhere. Let dry. Cover with a thin coat of decoupage glue.

4. Measure the inside of the box and cut decorative paper to fit. Glue the paper to the inside with decoupage glue. Let dry. Apply a thin coat of decoupage glue. Make a label with a scrap of decorative paper and the scallop scissors. Glue to the spine with white glue.

❖ ❖ ❖

MATERIALS

unpainted papier-mâché book box (available in craft stores)

white primer

decoupage glue

white tissue paper, cut into 2- and 3-inch pieces

decorative paper for covers

ecru paper for sides

decorative acid-free paper for lining

TOOLS

medium-size brush

X-Acto knife

metal-edged ruler

scallop-edged scissors

all-purpose white glue

themes: hobbies

Scrapbooks are a natural way to arrange, protect, and display family photos and memorabilia from special events or trips, but they are also a good place to organize information and notes about a favorite pastime. Hobbies such as gardening or birding easily lend themselves to—indeed, almost necessitate—journal-keeping, providing a place to keep detailed, illustrated records about your pursuit.

Sports

For a student athlete, collect team pictures, newspaper clippings, team rosters, home/away schedules, pep rally flyers, and details of the winning home run or game-saving touchdown. Be sure to include candid shots of the player in uniform on the field, whether celebrating a win or planning new strategies after a loss. For individual sports, such as gymnastics, ice skating, or swimming, include information about personal best times and scores, training schedules, and a "typical" day in the life of the athlete. Record impressions of those 5 A.M. trips to the rink now, while they're fresh in your memory.

Perhaps your enthusiasm comes from watching rather than participating in sports. If you follow a baseball, hockey, or football team, collect newspaper and magazine clippings about favorite players, box scores, and scouting reports plus stadium souvenirs such as score cards, ticket stubs, and game programs. A season's scrapbook makes a thoughtful gift for a dyed-in-the-wool fan who has moved out of the area. Make a cover for the album out of a collage of player cards (just not the valuable ones!).

Home Improvement

If your house is your hobby, whether by choice or necessity, keep details of past, present, and hoped-for projects in a journal or scrapbook. This type of book can take more than one format. If you live in a historic home, or are planning major renovations, keep "before and after" records to show to visiting friends and family. Such a book might also highlight information about the house's history and the major work undertaken, with photos, blueprints, wallpaper samples, and paint chips.

A work-in-progress journal, on the other hand, serves as a more practical homeowner's manual. In it you can keep a record of paint colors, appliance model numbers, and carpet and fabric patterns for future touch-ups or repairs. Also include magazine articles depicting projects or decorating styles that appeal to you, notes on materials purchased, invoices, service contracts, and guarantees.

Antiquing Adventures

There's plenty of scrapbooking material that can be gained from perusing tag sales, flea markets, and country auctions. You can find antique papers and decorations to include in a scrapbook, or, if you're a weekend flea-market fanatic, make a scrapbook to keep records of jaunts. If you're dedicated to collecting items of a particular theme, whether it be Depression glass, ironstone dishware, or baby dolls, use your scrapbook to record notes about price and condition information from published manuals in comparison with details of your expeditions.

Textile Art and Needlework

If you spend spare moments piecing quilt squares or designing counted cross-stitch samplers, use a scrapbook to save designs of projects you have completed as well as ones you are contemplating. Include swatches of fabric, snippets of thread and trimmings, photographs of finished masterpieces, stories of the origins of patterns, and notes about the handcrafted pieces you give as gifts. A scrapbook can also make a visually interesting gift for a hobbyist—perhaps an album with a quilted cover created from paper cutouts in a classic pattern (Tumbling Blocks or Log Cabin).

storing paper collectibles

◆ For best long-term preservation, handle paper collectibles carefully, especially if you are collecting as an investment rather than for pure sentiment. To maintain monetary value, comic books, magazines, trading cards, postcards, and the like should be in the best condition possible, with no bent corners or creases.

◆ Store in a cool, dark place that's not subject to dramatic fluctuations of temperature and humidity. Most garages, basements, and attics are not good spots.

◆ Don't use rubber bands or paper clips to hold items together. Rubber bands will eventually disintegrate and can leave behind residue that will harm paper; paper clips leave impressions in paper and metal ones usually rust eventually, too. Don't use cellophane tape on paper you wish to save.

◆ If you store magazines or comic books flat, alternate the direction of the spines.

◆ Consider packaging magazines or comics individually (or two or three together) in non-PVC plastic bags. Include a backing board (piece of cardboard; acid-free boards are available from suppliers of archival materials) with each bag for support.

gardener's workbook

When it's updated each season, this book will become a valuable record and workbook for the avid gardener, recording permanently the details of the evolution of a garden—the dates of the first frost, the first blossoms on a favorite tree, the times when a border is in bloom and when it looks bare. Use it to save garden plans, photographs, magazine clippings, and seed packets along with notes about planting dates, successful (or not) spots for plants, and ideas for future plantings. This book has tab dividers to separate the seasons or different areas of the garden.

1. With the hole punch, make five evenly spaced holes down a short side of each sheet of paper, about ¾ inch from the edge.

2. With the mat knife and ruler, cut two 11- by 8 ½-inch pieces of bristol board for the covers. Center one sheet of the hole-punched craft paper on a piece of bristol board and use it as a template to punch the cover holes. Repeat with the other piece of bristol board.

3. On one of the cover pieces, draw a light line 1 ¾ inches in from the same side you have hole punched. This will be the underside (inside) of the front cover. With the X-Acto knife and ruler, score partway through the bristol board (be careful not to cut all the way through) from top to bottom. Turn the board over and bend the board forward to create a crease.

4. Cut two 12 ½- by 10-inch pieces of the decorative paper. Spray the wrong side of one piece with adhesive. Position the front bristol board cover, with the fold face down, on the paper. Press to adhere. To make a mitered corner, diagonally trim the corners of the paper, to about ¼ inch from the corner of the board. Fold the edges of the paper over the board and press to adhere. Let dry. Repeat with the

MATERIALS

33 sheets (8 ½ by 11 inches) brown craft paper

large sheet (at least 20 by 30 inches) bristol board

large sheet (40 by 50 inches) decorative paper (hand-painted paper, wallpaper, or wrapping paper)

small sheet green corrugated cardboard

1 yard green twine

TOOLS

5/16-inch hole punch

mat knife

metal-edged ruler

X-Acto knife

spray adhesive or rubber cement

zigzag-edged scissors

second sheet of paper and the back cover. Punch holes through the paper at the bristol board holes.

5. Cut two 9- by 8-inch pieces of decorative paper with the zigzag scissors for the end sheets. Spray one with adhesive and position on the inside front cover, covering the edges on three sides but leaving the side with the holes open. Press to adhere. Repeat with the second piece of paper on the inside back cover.

6. Cut two $1\frac{1}{2}$- by $8\frac{1}{2}$-inch strips of corrugated cardboard. Use the cover as a template to mark where the five holes should be punched. Punch the holes. Assemble the book with the paper between the covers and the cardboard strips on the front and back covers. You may need to poke a pencil through the holes to line up all the elements.

7. Knot an end of the twine and whipstitch down the edge of the book, starting at the top (in the hole, through the back, and wrapping around the edge to the front, back into the next hole). When you get to the bottom, lace back up to the top again, using the same holes. When you get to the top, pull the twine tightly and knot in the back of the book. Cut the excess.

8. For the inside tabs, cut four $1\frac{1}{2}$- by 2-inch pieces of corrugated cardboard. Trim the short ends with the zigzag scissors. Lightly score each piece in half on the corrugated side and fold. Staple to the edge of a page and add a label below it. Repeat to make more tabs.

9. Make a label for the front cover with corrugated cardboard and decorative paper trimmed with the zigzag scissors. Glue to the front of the book.

❖   ❖   ❖

For people of a certain age, there comes a time when closets and drawers are already burgeoning with enough neckties, spanking-new unworn shirts, and perfume bottles to last seemingly forever. Instead of these familiar presents, commemorate a milestone birthday, anniversary, or retirement with a handcrafted memory book sure to be among the most thoughtful and appreciated of gifts.

If you have access to a good supply of photos and memorabilia, you may choose to craft the book independently, start to finish. A collaborative effort, however, can add to the project and be a lot of fun for all involved. In either case, the final effort will be enjoyed by the recipient over and over again.

Compiling a book filled with testimonials and memories from relatives, childhood friends, or business associates will take a bit of planning. Well in advance of the special day, contact friends and family members and request their help. Ask them to send along memorabilia such as photographs, ticket stubs, newspaper clippings, birth announcements, and graduation programs. Ask for anecdotes or testimonials. (Be sure to include a deadline for returning materials.) Then, assemble the materials yourself, retyping or handwriting anecdotes and mounting photos so the style of the book will be consistent from start to finish.

Alternatively, you can send each potential participant an envelope filled with a kit consisting of one or two memory book pages, photo corners or photo sleeves, and anything else you wish. Then it becomes a simple matter for you to assemble finished pages into a book. At the party, you might want to have each participant "present" his or her page to the guest of honor and describe a few of the entries for the crowd. If there's time, have people send the pages to you in advance; you'd be wise, however, to choose a format that will allow you to include any last-minute masterpieces that may be delivered directly to the party. Make it clear if the project is to be a surprise!

MEMORY BOOK THEMES

◆ For newlyweds or newly engaged: Gather childhood photos of the couple as well as pictures from when they began dating.

◆ For silver or golden anniversaries: Relatives and friends who attended the wedding just may have snapshots that the anniversary couple have never seen. If you can get copies of the photographs, you may add a whole new dimension to their memory of that special day. Also include anecdotes from friends who may remember when the couple first fell in love, as well as stories and family lore from the couple's children, grandchildren, and nieces and nephews.

◆ For a graduation: Proud graduates of any age from preschool to doctorate will treasure a book filled with photos of the honoree and friends (if your own archives are short on these photos, ask friends to contribute images), and, if possible, photos of teachers. This is a good place to make use of some of those school papers and artwork you've been saving all these years!

◆ For a concert or recital: Mark an important public concert with a small memory book. Include photographs of the performer as a budding young artist. Create a frame for the song list or recital program; and collect as many programs and newspaper reviews as you can from throughout the years. Layer a page with cutout snippets of the piece they performed. If your performer has a musical hero or heroine, include silhouetted images—perhaps as a backdrop to a page—of this influential person. This project would also be a nice memento for an art exhibit or dance recital.

◆ For a milestone birthday: Contact childhood friends for school-day stories. At the

a birthday party album

The cake, the candles, the balloons and streamers, the presents . . . there's a certain similarity to the ingredients for a happy birthday party whether you're in California or Connecticut. But a birthday album can be unique, and offer an occasion to play with the way photos are displayed and embellished.

◆ Photos don't have to be laid out in straight rows. Cut out circles of colored paper (or use purchased die-cut balloon shapes) and put a trimmed photo of a party-goer into the center of each balloon.

◆ Or, decorate around each photo to make it look like a birthday present. Young children like "lift-the-flap" page papercutouts shaped like presents that can be "opened" to reveal a party photo underneath.

◆ Experiment with matching or contrasting preprinted scrapbook paper as an alternative to plain white or black pages. Choose paper with favorite cartoon characters for a child's page; a floral background for the avid gardener; a sophisticated marbleized paper for a grown-up.

◆ For a child's birthday book, embellish the page with stickers, die-cut shapes, or your own sketches to recall the party's theme of dinosaurs, clowns, or princesses.

local library, try looking up a microfilm version of the newspaper from the person's date of birth and print out some of the top stories of the day. If it's feasible, include vintage snapshots beside modern-day photos of the person's childhood home, school, church, college, first job site, etc.

◆ For a retirement party: Collect stories from colleagues at the current job as well as from any special people at past places of employment. Keep in mind that the retiree-to-be may have mixed emotions, from jubilation to trepidation to bittersweet anticipation of the newly found "free" time soon to begin. Make the occasion a time to toast the retiree's future as well as celebrate the past.

◆ "This is Your Life": A birth-till-now book can be great fun for compilers and recipient alike. You'll need to have a pretty good outline of milestones in the person's life, which can include the obvious birth, school, and employment history plus details of marriage and children; but don't forget trivia such as information about the childhood family pet, favorite ice cream store, and other minutiae of day-to-day life.

folk art freedom

Sometimes grown-ups get too caught up in minuscule details and the search for unattainable—and ultimately unimportant—perfection. There's nothing like working alongside a child to give you a fresh perspective.

Morna Crites-Moore designed the Holiday Memory Book (page 105) based on a Christmas picture drawn by her 11-year-old daughter Jessica. The simplified shapes of the child's drawing translate beautifully into the folk-art style cover, pieced from homemade felt and embellished with buttons and bits of silk. Crites-Moore finds that working with her daughter frees her from being overly judgmental and encourages a willingness to experiment with different artistic techniques.

Folk art's character, after all, depends for its beauty not on "perfection" but on the sheer pleasure of color, shape, and texture working together to create a harmonious, homey whole. Stitches can be visible or uneven; shapes may be a little irregular. The result is perfect in its own way, especially for a subject as personal and idiosyncratic as scrapbooking.

HOLIDAY MEMORIES

Whether you take a religious or secular approach to Hanukkah, Kwanzaa, Chinese New Year, or Christmas, the spirit of giving and a childlike wonder at the season's miracles are at the heart of the festivities. Expectations of the season's pleasures, for many people, are linked back to their very earliest memories, and traditions you establish now will stay with your children for a lifetime. In the spirit of remembering holidays past, honoring the present, and looking forward to holidays in the future, create a special holiday memory book to share with your family.

Just as the future is unwritten, you need only begin this book with a pleasing cover and blank pages to be completed with each passing year. This year, for example, you can begin with a few photographs marking your family's own holiday celebrations, whether you're out chopping down a fresh tree, lighting the menorah, preparing a traditional meal, or gathered around the fireplace hanging stockings. Add some drawings from the children, menus for holiday meals, a page from a holiday concert program, favorite cards or wrapping paper, tracings of your favorite cookie cutters—whatever strikes your fancy. Establish a tradition of taking a group photograph of family and friends around the tree. In years to come this makes a fascinating time line.

At the close of the holiday season, wrap the book carefully and store it with your holiday decorations. As it's brought out each year, your family's happy times will be recalled, relived, documented, and enriched.

special birthday
scrapbook

This beautiful fabric-covered book could be adapted for a family history book (use a family plaid or a rich-colored bookbinding cloth) or a baby book (cover a bright fabric with tiny buttons, or a printed fabric with miniature silk daisies). Here, velvet dressed with silk flowers suits this milestone birthday album. Choose a stable cotton velvet rather than a stretchy velour for best results.

1. Cut out the elements of the scrapbook: With the mat knife and ruler, cut two 10-inch-square cover boards and two 1- by 10-inch fastening flaps from the chipboard. To cover the boards, cut two 13 3/4- by 12-inch pieces of velvet and two 10-inch squares of batting. For the end sheets, cut two 11-inch squares of raw silk. For the end sheet linings, cut two 9 1/2-inch squares of poster board. To cover the fastening flaps, cut two 4- by 11-inch strips of raw silk. For the pages, cut about 12 pieces of heavy-weight paper, 9 3/4 by 9 1/2 inches.

2. With the awl, make two holes in the center of each fastening flap, 2 inches in from each end and wide enough to allow the screw fasteners to fit snugly into them. Use one flap as a template and mark on a page where the holes should go. Punch holes in the paper with the awl, three or four pages at a time.

3. With the fabric glue, glue the batting to the cover boards. Let dry. Spray adhesive to the batting side of a cover board. Carefully position the board on the wrong side of a piece of velvet, leaving 1-inch margins on three sides and a 2 3/4-inch margin on the fourth side. Spray adhesive on one side of a fastening flap and place on the wide margin, 3/4 inch from the cover board and 1 inch from the edge. Repeat with the second cover board, flap, and piece of velvet.

MATERIALS

large sheet (at least 16 by 20 inches) chipboard

1/2 yard velvet fabric

batting

1/2 yard raw silk fabric

sheet light-gauge poster board or heavy paper

2 or 3 large (20 by 30 inches) sheets heavy-weight paper

screw fasteners (the type used in photo albums)

silk flowers

TOOLS

mat knife

metal-edged ruler

awl

fabric glue

spray adhesive

4. To make a mitered corner, diagonally trim the corners of the velvet, to about 1/4 inch from the corner of the board. Apply fabric glue to the board edges and fold the velvet over. Press to adhere.

5. Fold in the edges of the two 11-inch squares of raw silk 3/4 inch, creating 9 1/2-inch squares. Miter the corners neatly. Press with a warm iron. Fit one poster board liner inside each piece of pressed silk.

6. On each of the 4- by 11-inch strips of raw silk, fold the long edges in by 1/2 inch and the short edges in by 3/4 inch, creating 3- by 9 1/2-inch strips. Miter the corners and iron flat. With the velvet-covered side face down, center the silk strip over the fastening flap (it has the two holes that will hold the fasteners) so that a 1/4-inch border is left on top, bottom, and one side. Approximately 1 inch of fabric will be covering the flap; the remaining 2 inches of fabric will overlap onto the inside front cover. Glue the silk strip to the flap and inside front cover by spreading a thin layer of fabric glue on the cover and then positioning the fabric. Repeat for the back flap.

7. Center and glue the silk-covered panel on the inside cover, leaving a 1/4-inch border. With the awl, carefully open the holes in the silk on the fastening flaps of the front and back covers.

8. Assemble the album with the pages between the covers. Insert the fasteners through the holes in the flaps. Screw the fasteners tight. With the fabric glue, glue silk flowers to the front of the album.

❖   ❖   ❖

Remember when...

Mother bought us new Easter outfits
so we could have our picture taken.
We had an easter egg hunt and got all
muddy! Mother was mad, but soon forgave
us, and we then opned our baskets.

Remember whe...

I'll never forget the time Grandm...
brought us to ice skate in Rocke...
Center! We had hot chocolat...
warm us up! It wa...
except when Gra...

This seasonal fabric design transforms a store-bought scrapbook into a memory book for the holidays. At the end of the season, wrap this charming book in a length of muslin or a Christmas-print fabric and store it with your Christmas decorations. Taking it out each year and looking over photographs while adding new ones will become a much-loved holiday ritual for your family.

1. Cut a 14-inch square of muslin to serve as a base for the front cover. Cut a 10-inch square of white felted wool to serve as the central background. Tack it to the center of the muslin piece. The muslin backing will serve as a place to anchor stitches without worrying about marring the appearance of the front cover.

2. Cut tree and trunk shapes from green and brown felted wool. Using wool tapestry yarn, sew to the background, tucking the trunk underneath the tree.

3. To make garlands, cut tiny scraps of wool in a variety of colors. String the wool, along with buttons and bells, onto embroidery floss. Make several short garland pieces and arrange them on the tree. When you are satisfied with the placement, tack them down with sewing thread. Sew on beads and buttons (the tiniest buttons can be found where doll-sized supplies are sold) to decorate the tree. Embellish the background with randomly scattered cross-stitches and French knots of wool thread.

4. Cut two cat shapes from felted wool and place one on each side of the tree. Sew around the edges with wool thread. Paint on the eyes and stitch embroidery floss for the whiskers.

5. Make little gift boxes to place under the tree with two or three

MATERIALS

13- by 12 1/2-inch scrapbook

muslin or other cotton fabric, to use as a base for sewing

felted wool from old sweaters and blankets (see page 107), or purchased felt

various weights of threads (sewing thread, embroidery floss, wool tapestry thread, gold metallic thread)

beads and buttons in various sizes

tiny bells (available at craft stores)

acrylic paint for cats' eyes

cardboard

necktie and other fabric scraps

scraps of thin ribbon

1 yard red wool cord or piping

TOOLS

tiny paint brush ('000' spotting brush works best)

tapestry needles

pieces of 1-inch-square cardboard taped together. Wrap them with small scraps of a necktie or velvet and sew the wrapping together where you would ordinarily use tape. Repeat to make more gifts of different sizes. Use embroidery floss, metallic gold thread, or gold silk ribbon as ribbons for the gifts. Arrange the gift boxes under the tree and tack them in place.

6. Cut four $1/4$-inch-wide strips, 10 inches long, of black felted wool to make a border around the picture. Sew to the muslin, catching the white felt as well.

7. Cut four $1 1/2$-inch-wide strips, 10 inches long, of green felted wool for the frame. Lay the strips in place and stitch them to the black strips, leaving the corners empty. Cut four $1 1/2$-inch squares of different shades of brown felted wool and sew in place in the corners.

8. To make the book cover (somewhat like the book covers you made in high school), open up the scrapbook and center it on a large piece of felted wool—at least 55 by 14 inches. If you don't have a piece that large, join two pieces together by butting the edges together and joining them with a zigzag stitch. Fold the wool around the closed book, with the ends folded over the covers to the inside (check that there is enough slack to open and close the book properly). Pin in place, then sew around the edges of the book. Remove the pins. Trim the edges.

9. Place the muslin-felt cover piece on the front cover and sew in place, around the edge. Cut an 82-inch length of red piping and, with wool thread, sew it around the outside edge of the front and back covers. Cut off any excess. Cut two 24-inch lengths of piping. Sew one length of piping along the front joint (where the spine meets the cover) from the bottom to the middle. Sew the other length from the top to the middle. Tie the free ends in a bow.

❖   ❖   ❖

felted wool

Felted wool is made from old sweaters, blankets, and other wool items. When wool is subjected to heat, soap, and agitation, the fibers shrink and form a dense piece of felt. Like store-bought felt, the fabric does not need hems.

◆ Choose old sweaters or blankets that are 100 percent wool. Wool that is labeled "washable," will not shrink. Wash similar colors together since dyes may bleed.

◆ Wash the wool pieces with detergent and hot water several times on the roughest agitation cycle your machine has. Once the sweaters have gone through three or four wash cycles, they will be as felted as they are likely to get. Keep in mind that different kinds of wool will felt differently, some more than others.

◆ Dry the wool on the dryer's hot setting. Cut out the seam lines and steam-iron the fabric to create flat pieces of felt wool.

resources

ADVENTURES IN CRAFTS
P.O. Box 6058 Yorkville Station
New York, NY 10128
(212) 410-9793
unfinished wood shadow boxes

ANTIQUE HARDWARE AND HOME
19 Buckingham Plantation Drive
Bluffton, SC 29910
(800) 422-9982
www.authentictreasures.com
shadow boxes

BALLARD DESIGNS
catalog, (800) 367-2775
curio cabinets for shadow boxes

BOOKMAKERS INTERNATIONAL
6001 66th Avenue
Suite 100
Riverdale, MD 20737
(301) 459-3384
Bookbinding supplies; specialty paper

CANSON-TALENS, INC.
21 Industrial Drive
South Hadley, MA 01075
(413) 538-9250
www.canson-us.com
archival art and craft paper

CUT IT UP
P.O. Box 287
Gold Run, CA 95717
(530) 389-2233
www.scrapramento.com
full range of scrapbook supplies, including stickers, punches, templates, albums, die-cut paper shapes, how-to books

DECORATOR AND CRAFT CORPORATION
428 South Zelta
Wichita, KS 67207
(800) 835-3013
papier-mâché memory boxes

DEJAVIEWS
6 Britton Drive
Bloomfield, CT 06002
(800) 243-8419
www.cthruruler.com
plastic templates, edging tools, see-through rulers, stamp positioners, memory boxes

DICK BLICK ART MATERIALS
P.O. Box 1267
695 Route 150
Galesburg, IL 61402
(800) 447-8192
www.dickblick.com
full range of arts and craft supplies

EXPOSURES
catalog, (800) 572-5750
acid-free scrapbooks, photo albums, shadow boxes, storage boxes

FISKARS, INC.
P.O. Box 8027
Wausau, WI 54402
(800) 950-0203
www.fiskars.com
full range of scrapbook supplies, including specialty scissors, kits, boxes, albums, booklets

FRANCES MEYER, INC.
P.O. Box 3088
Savannah, GA 31402
(800) FRANCES
www.francesmeyer.com
full range of scrapbook supplies, including starter kits, stickers, binders, patterned paper

KATE'S PAPERIE
561 Broadway
New York, NY 10012
(212) 941-9816
catalog, (800) 809-9880
handmade and exotic papers

LIGHT IMPRESSIONS
P.O. Box 940
Rochester, NY 14603-0940
(800) 828-6216
www.lightimpressionsdirect.com
archival supplies, including deacidifying solutions, albums, frames, mat board, storage boxes

LOOSE ENDS
P.O. Box 20310
Keizer, OR 97307
(503) 390-7457
www.4loosends.com
handmade papers

M & J TRIMMING CO.
1008 Avenue of the Americas
New York, NY 10018
(212) 391-6200
ribbons, trim

MRS. GROSSMAN'S
3810 Cypress Drive
Petaluma, CA 94954
(800) 457-4570
www.mrsgrossmans.com
stickers, scrapbooks, scrapbook kits, idea books

NEW YORK CENTRAL ART SUPPLY
62 Third Avenue
New York, NY 10003
(800) 950-6111
www.nycentralart.com
bookbinding fabric, large selection of specialty papers, photo albums

PEARL PAINT
308 Canal Street
New York, NY 10013
catalog, (800) 221-6845 ext. 2297
www.pearlpaint.com
full range of arts and craft supplies

PLAID ENTERPRISES
1649 International Court
Norcross, GA 30091
(800) 842-4197
www.plaidonline.com
Folk Art acrylic paint and Royal Coat Decoupage Finish; paint dotters, rollers, stamps, stencils

QUEEN CITY PAPER
5 Floridian Drive
Erlanger, KY 41018
(800) 669-2400
www.queencitymatboard.com
acid-free decorative mat board and chip board

RESOURCE INTERNATIONAL
(888) 927-9052
acid-free fiberboard boxes

SAKURA
(800) 776-6257
www.gellyroll.com
archival rollerball pens

TALAS
568 Broadway
New York, NY 10012
(212) 219-0770
www.talas-nyc.com
bookbinding supplies including bookbinding board and fabric, paper, conservation supplies

UNIVERSITY PRODUCTS, INC.
517 Main Street
P.O. Box 101
Holyoke, MA 01041-0101
(800) 628-1912
www.universityproducts.com
archival-quality supplies, including albums, pages, mat board, adhesives, storage boxes, deacidifying solutions

WALNUT HOLLOW
1409 State Road 23
Dodgeville, WI 53533-2112
(800) 950-5101
www.walnuthollow.com
memory boxes and wooden albums

index

Acknowledgments

The author would like to thank:
Ray DiGiovanni, Hot Shots Photo Lab, Stratford, Connecticut; Lesley
Finch, floral designer, Norwalk, Connecticut; Alyce Parseghian, artist/
photographer, Franklin Lakes, New Jersey; Jo Shields, Shields & Partners,
Westport, Connecticut

Crafts and how-to instructions on pages 35, 49, and 84 by Susan Mills;
pages 39, 64, and 88 by Robin Tarnoff; pages 45 and 73 by Ellen Goldberg;
page 53 by Karen Silver Bloom; page 60 by Petra Boase; pages 68 and 77 by
Allison Meyler; pages 80 and 101 by Maria Kessel; page 92 by Amy Leonard;
page 105 by Morna and Jessica Crites-Moore